CHRISTIANITY
IN
THE UNITED
STATES

EARLE E. CAIRNS

CHRISTIANITY

in

THE UNITED STATES

CHRISTIANITY
in
THE UNITED STATES

By

1344

EARLE E. CAIRNS

*Chairman of the Department of History
and Political Science,
Wheaton College*

MOODY PRESS
CHICAGO

Library of Congress Catalog Card Number: 64-20990

Printed in the United States of America

CONTENTS

FROM SCHISM AND IDEALISM
TO ABSOLUTISM AND ECUMENICALISM
(1877-Present)

LIST OF DIAGRAMS

PREFACE

THIS STORY of the churches in our land links information and interpretation in an organized pattern in which religion is seen in its historical setting. In this way religious history is not treated in a historical vacuum. Bibliography at the end of each chapter is arranged according to the order of topics in the chapter. It includes both primary sources and the better secondary accounts. Page references in the texts by Olmstead and Sweet are cited in each chapter.

The curious minds and interest of the author's students in American church history have resulted over the years in much of whatever is worthwhile in this book. An expression of gratitude to Professor Timothy Smith for his helpful counsel in organizing this work and to my colleague Professor Hudson T. Armerding for taking the time to read and comment helpfully on the manuscript is also in order. My wife has served as an able and constructive critic at each step. The careful work of my assistant, Howard A. Whaley, in checking the bibliography and of his wife in typing the final draft of the manuscript is greatly appreciated.

The author hopes that this book may help many Americans to become aware of their great spiritual heritage. Many enemies, external and internal, would destroy our political freedom, which is so closely related to our religious heritage. Only a return to faith in the God of the founders of religion in this land will guide our country through crisis and fit it for the work of world leadership in this century.

INTRODUCTION

RELIGIOUS PLURALISM is both the pride and problem of American Christianity. This multiplying of religious organizations is the outcome of the religious heritage from Europe and the modifying influence of the American environment. It has been coupled with separation of church and state and full religious liberty, which permits freedom of conscience to all. Interfaith competition has also contributed to the vitality and creativity of Christianity in America. Freedom and individualism have replaced the authoritarianism and institutionalism of Europe.

This *creativity* has been evidenced in several ways. Churches in America have pioneered in various types of youth work. From the creation of Christian Endeavor in 1881 to nondenominational youth organizations, such as the worldwide Youth for Christ, and denominational groups, such as the Lutheran Walther League or the Methodist Epworth League, this tendency has been prominent.

The institutional church was developed in the last century to solve the problems of the flight of prosperous middle-class parishioners to the suburbs from the downtown churches and the needs of the poorer people in the area by organizing churches which would minister to the whole man—body, soul and spirit— with gymnasiums, chapels, vocational classes, child care instruction, handicrafts and other activities. City missions were organized also to meet the needs of the down-and-outs both for temporal and spiritual food and to help restore them to society.

Churches in no other country except Britain have been more generous in contributions to missionary work and philanthropic activities. The American churches after World War II contributed more than one hundred million dollars to the reconstruction of churches in war-torn areas of Europe and Asia. Wherever there has been human need, there has been a generous response to meet the need. It should be borne in mind that this giving has been voluntary and apart from any system of forced church tithes or church taxes.

Consideration of the *characteristics* of Christianity in this country also demonstrates this vitality and creativity. Religious pluralism in the form of denominationalism has flowered most fully in the United States, which has more than two hundred fifty religious bodies. Both the religious radicalism of many of the early colonists and the accessibility of empty space on the frontier helped to promote this trend. Religious pluralism has promoted freedom of conscience and a spirit of toleration and ecumenicity.

The absence of an established or state church has promoted voluntarism and the participation of the laity in the affairs of the church in a way unprecedented in Europe. The Separatist concept of the free congregation and the idea of a pure or regenerate church membership linked in a church covenant stimulated these ideas.

Perhaps it was the absence of a state church into which one was born and the masses brought in by migration that have made revivalism and evangelism so characteristic of American Christianity. If people were to be brought under the influence of Christianity it would have to be by persuasion. The frontier camp meeting is one such illustration of this approach.

Europeans have often commented on the activism and pragmatism of the church in the United States, which have been evidenced in such movements as the Social Gospel. Perhaps these characteristics account for the fact that there have been few outstanding American theologians.

One is also impressed with the ecumenical spirit of American Christianity from the days when Zinzendorf tried to unite the German churches of Pennsylvania to the present powerful ecumenical movement. Leadership in both conservative and liberal ecumenical movements throughout the world has come from this country.

The environment of the New World also produced an optimism which put eschatology in a secondary place. This optimism was evidenced in the perfectionist groups of the mid-nineteenth century and is seen in the present leadership in missions and the ecumenical movement.

What *reasons* account for the creativity and dynamic characteristics of American Christianity? Certainly the frontier provided space for people to try experiments which might not have been acceptable in a more crowded society. The frontiersman has always been individualistic and impatient with external authority.

One must not forget the relative radicalism of many of the

groups which migrated to this land to get away from established authority. This radicalism was political, social and theological. Often in the colonies no one group was strong enough to dominate, and practical toleration of each other became a necessity. Roger Williams and William Penn adopted policies of full freedom of conscience with no established church and promoted immigration to their colonies. Negative factors, such as the lack of restraint from an established church and the distance from England both in terms of miles and time, promoted free expression of religious ideals.

From the earliest revivals to the present, revivalism has often been the source of new denominations, practices and theological concepts. Jonathan Edwards thought creatively in order to link the revivalism of the Great Awakening with Calvinistic theology. The camp meeting was another creative result of the Second Awakening in the United States.

The problem of slavery forced creative thought and activity upon the churches of the North and South during the midnineteenth century. Negro Christianity has developed many unique methods of religious expression. New Negro denominations emerged before and after the Civil War.

The spirit of nationalism which came out of the Revolutionary War led to the creation of nationwide denominations which were completely divorced from their counterparts in England and on the Continent. The First Amendment to the Constitution forbade the setting up of a privileged, preferred or state church.

The pragmatic and activistic spirit of religious bodies in our land must enter into any consideration of religious creativity. Christians in the United States have demonstrated more of the Martha than the Mary spirit. The Social Gospel is but one evidence of this.

Modern religious ecumenicalism may question whether or not our religious pluralism has been an unmixed blessing, but its *sources* can be readily observed. Old World theological and ethnic denominational groups brought their differences with them when they migrated. Frontier Christianity produced Mormon and Adventist groups, and the city has contributed such cults as Christian Science. Disagreement over doctrine and liturgy led to the emergence of the Orthodox Presbyterian and Reformed Episcopal churches. Revivalism brought into being the Cumberland Presbyterian church when the parent body could find in it no room for untrained but zealous preachers. The slavery conflict created Negro churches and divisions which have not yet been healed in the Presbyterian and Baptist communions. Above all, religious liberty has left the way open for varied expressions of the religious spirit.

It is interesting to note that the discovery of the New World by Columbus coincided with the breakup of the static, corporate, institutionalized universal religion of medieval Europe and the emergence of new national Protestant churches which provided the bulk of the migrants to the United States. This heritage with the stimulus of the frontier in a new open land provided a setting in which Christianity could manifest itself in new ways. The story of the importation and transplanting of European Christianity and its modification in the new environment is the theme of this book.

GENERAL BIBLIOGRAPHY

Bibliographies:

CASE, SHIRLEY J. (ed.). *A Bibliographical Guide to the History of Christianity.* Chicago: University of Chicago Press, 1931.

HANDLIN, OSCAR, *et al. Harvard Guide to American History.* Cambridge: Harvard University Press, 1954. Contains scattered bibliographic items pertaining to American religious history.

Sources:

COMMAGER, HENRY S. *Documents of American History* (6th ed.). New York: Appleton-Century-Crofts, Inc., 1958. Has many documents pertaining to religious history.

MODE, PETER G. *Sourcebook and Bibliographical Guide to American Church History.* Menasha, Wis.: George Banta Publishing Co., 1921. Useful bibliography. Excellent collection of documents in this now out-of-print work.

SMITH, H. SHELTON, HANDY, ROBERT T., and LOETSCHER, LEFFERTS A. *American Christianity.* 2 vols. New York: Charles Scribner's Sons, 1961-1963. Documents coupled with interpretation and bibliography make this a useful work.

SMITH, JAMES W., and JAMISON, A. LELAND (eds.). *Religion in American Life.* Vols. 1, 2, 4. Princeton: Princeton University Press, 1961. Excellent interpretive and historical essays on various phases of American religious life with extensive critical and annotated bibliographical notes. Volume 3 to be published later.

Histories of American Christianity:

BACON, LEONARD W. *A History of American Christianity.* New York: Christian Literature Co., 1897. An early history of American Christianity in the American Church History Series edited by Philip Schaff.

BEARDSLEY, FRANK G. *Christian Achievement in America.* Chicago: Winona Publishing Co., 1907.

——. *The History of Christianity in America.* New York: American Tract Society, 1938. Popular but fairly reliable survey.

BRAUER, JERALD C. *Protestantism in America.* Philadelphia: The Westminster Press, 1953. Useful and accurate survey of American religious history.

CURRAN, FRANCIS X. *Major Trends in American Church History.* New York: American Press, 1946. An able but often biased survey of American religious life from the Roman Catholic viewpoint.

DRUMMOND, ANDREW L. *Story of American Protestantism.* Edinburgh: Oliver and Boyd, 1949. Readable but not always accurate account of American Protestantism, for Englishmen by an Englishman.

GAUSTAD, EDWIN S. *Historical Atlas of American Religion.* New York: Harper & Row, 1962. Excellent historical survey illustrated with many fine maps, charts and graphs to show the growth of Christianity in the United States. Good bibliography.

HUDSON, WINTHROP S. *American Protestantism.* Chicago: University of Chicago Press, 1961. A discussion of the rise and decline of Protestant influence in American culture.

OLMSTEAD, CLIFTON E. *History of Religion in the United States.* Englewood Cliffs, N.J.: Prentice-Hall Inc., 1960. Excellent survey incorporating recent research. Designated hereafter as Olmstead, *HRUS.*

OSBORN, RONALD E. *The Spirit of American Christianity.* New York: Harper & Brothers, 1958. Brief interpretive survey of American religious history with useful insights.

ROWE, HENRY K. *The History of Religion in the United States.* New York: The Macmillan Co., 1924. Topical and chronological interpretation of the general significance of religion in American life.

SCHAFF, PHILIP, *et al. The American Church History Series.* 13 vols. New York: Christian Literature Co., 1893-1897. An early large-scale delineation of American religious history by authorities.

SCHLESINGER, ARTHUR M., and FOX, DIXON R. (eds.). *A History of American Life.* 12 vols. New York: The Macmillan Co., 1929-1930. Presentation in chronological sequence of useful data on religion in the era covered by each volume from Spanish missions to the New Deal.

SPERRY, WILLARD L. *Religion in America.* Cambridge: Cambridge University Press, 1946. American religious history interpreted by an American for Englishmen.

SWEET, WILLIAM W. *The Story of Religion in America* (rev.). New York: Harper & Brothers, 1950. The standard text in the field by an authority. Designated hereafter as Sweet, *SRA.* See Sweet, *SRA* 1-7 for data discussed in the introduction.

WEIGLE, LUTHER A. *American Idealism.* (*The Pageant of America,* edited by R. H. Gabriel.) New Haven: Yale University Press, Vol. X, 1928. Contains excellent pictures illuminating quotations from sources and a chronological-topical discussion of American church history.

History of Denominations:

FERM, VERGILIUS T. (ed.). *The American Church of the Protestant Heritage*. New York: Philosophical Library, 1953. Chapters by denominational experts on the Old World and American origins, history, theology and polity of the major denominations.

LANDIS, BENSON Y. (ed.). *Yearbook of American Churches*. New York: National Council of Churches, 1916-1960. Annual editions of this work give current information on denominations.

MEAD, FRANK S. *Handbook of Denominations in the United States*. (rev. and enl.). Nashville: Abingdon Press, 1956. Helpful on history and organization of leading denominations.

WILLIAMS, JOHN P. *What Americans Believe and How They Worship*. New York: Harper & Brothers, 1952.

Biographies:

The Dictionary of American Biography. Auspices of American Council of Learned Societies. New York: Charles Scribner's Sons, 1928-1936. An excellent source of biographical data.

MOYER, ELGIN S. *Who Was Who in Church History*. Chicago: Moody Press, 1962. Biographical sketches of individuals important in American church history.

SWEET, WILLIAM W. *Makers of Christianity*. New York: Henry Holt & Co., 1937. Short scholarly biographies of nearly forty of the major figures of American religious history.

AMERICAN RELIGION IN THE COLONIAL ERA

(1607-1775)

1

OLD-WORLD RELIGIOUS HERITAGE

CULTURE IN THIS LAND is a heritage from Europe. The United States is a part of the Atlantic community of nations. This common political system of liberty, social mobility, literature, such as the Bible, and the Christian faith have been modified by the environment. But they still link this nation with Europe and especially England. Christianity in the United States is a migratory transplant of the sixteenth century Reformation, the seventeenth century Puritan and Quaker movements, and the Enlightenment.

From the British Isles

It has been said that "gospel, gold and glory" were the motives leading men to the New World. Mercantilistic theory, a feature of which made ownership of bullion the key to national power, led men to seek gold in the New World. When gold could not be found in the great amounts that Spain secured from her empire, nations turned to colonies as a way to get a favorable trade balance. The economic motive certainly played an important part in colonization.

Ownership of colonies would also enhance the prestige of the motherland. Furthermore, colonies could be military bulwarks against a rival colonial power. Georgia, it was argued, would be a buffer against Spanish expansion to the north.

Religious motivation seems to have played an important role in migration. Examination of the early charters of English colonizing companies indicates that conversion of the aborigines was to be an important part of their work.[1] Many, like the Quakers, also came to the colonies to escape religious persecution or, like the Puritans of New England, to seek a place where they would be free to practice religion according to the dictates of their conscience.

Migration in the colonial era was, except for the Swedish and Dutch, primarily from the British Isles. Migration from the time of the Declaration of Independence to the closing of the frontier was mainly from Protestant Calvinistic middle-class northern and western Europe, but after 1890 it consisted mainly of Roman Catholic migrants from southern and eastern Europe.

The *Anglican church* provided both colonists and a state church for several colonies. The Continental Reformation was mainly a popular middle-class movement upholding the theology of a clerical leadership. The Reformation in England, however, began as a politico-ecclesiastical break with Rome under Henry VIII, became an ethical and theological movement under Edward VI, and was stabilized under Elizabeth with its Thirty-nine Articles and a prayer book. In order to have his hoped-for legitimate male heir by a new wife, Anne, it was necessary for Henry to divorce his former wife. When the Pope refused this, Henry secured the divorce from the English clergy and denied papal supremacy in England by the Act of Supremacy (1534), which made the king "the supreme head" of the church in England. That this was not a theological break was demonstrated by the Six Articles (1539), which were a parliamentary reassertion of transubstantiation and other basic Roman Catholic doctrines. The publication of the Great Bible in 1539 was Henry's sole concession to the Protestant spirit.

Under the leadership of Thomas Cranmer, archbishop of Canterbury, the Reformation became religious. He was responsible for the second prayer book of 1552 and had a large part under Edward in the drawing up of the Forty-two Articles, a moderately Calvinistic creed. Services in the church were to be in English rather than in Latin.

Mary tried to bring about a Counter-Reformation which would turn the religious clock in England back to the time before Henry's quarrel with the Pope. But her marriage to Philip II of Spain and particularly her persecution of the Protestants turned the English toward Protestantism. Nearly three

---

[1] Peter G. Mode, *Sourcebook and Bibliographical Guide to American Church History* (Menasha, Wis.: George Banta Publishing Co., 1921), pp. 9, 12.

hundred, mainly from southern England, lost their lives in the fires of martyrdom. When she replaced her half-sister in 1558, Elizabeth determined to have a moderate settlement. The Forty-two Articles were compressed to Thirty-nine Articles and the prayer book was adopted. This state church in England was to become the established church in six of the thirteen colonies.

Several groups, however, were not satisfied with this settlement and began to agitate for a purified Anglican church. The *Puritan* movement developed after 1560. Some Puritans under the leadership of Thomas Cartwright desired a transformation of the Anglican church into a Presbyterian state church. Other Puritans, such as the Congregationalist Henry Jacobs, wanted a Congregational state church in which each congregation would have freedom to determine its own affairs. Still other Separatist Puritans held that each local church must be autonomous, select its own minister, conduct its own affairs, and be made up of a body of believers united to one another and to Christ by a voluntary church covenant. This concept was enunciated by Robert Browne in his *Reformation Without Tarrying for Anie*. It was the Separatist congregation at Scrooby which, because of persecution, moved to Leyden, Holland, and later back to Plymouth, England. Members of this group were the passengers which came to Plymouth on the "Mayflower" in 1620.

While these Puritans differed with each other on polity, they agreed on a common dislike of liturgy and the prayer book, on the final authority of the Bible, Sabbatarianism and a Calvinistic covenant theology which was expressed in such creeds as the Westminster Confession and the Savoy Declaration. Their struggle for their faith became a part of the struggle in the seventeenth century between the forces of the Parliament and the king. The House of Commons claimed sovereignty over legislation and finance, which the king claimed were his prerogatives. When Charles I ruled from 1629 to 1639 without a Parliament, many of the Puritans decided to migrate. About twenty thousand went to New England and another twenty thousand to the Caribbean. This struggle against an episcopal state church and a divine right monarchy in an era of political ferment meant that the things for which they were fighting—responsible self-government, individual rights and sovereignty of the people—were carried by them to the New World and applied with modifications in their colonies. Thus Congregationalism became the established church of Massachusetts, Connecticut and New Hampshire.

The *Quakers* formed another radical group. Their leader, George Fox, and his follower, Robert Barclay, the theologian of the group, emphasized the inner light as a primary source of revelation by the Holy Spirit to the individual. This was subject only to the secondary revelation of the Bible and of reason. Their refusal to doff their hats to superiors, to take oaths and to serve in the armed forces made them the subject of English persecution after 1660. They constituted a large percentage of the colonists who settled in New Jersey and Pennsylvania.

The *Scotch-Irish* formed still another important element of population in the thirteen colonies. James I, after a serious rebellion of the Irish in the latter years of Elizabeth's reign, formed a "plantation" in northern Ireland, or Ulster, and transplanted Scottish Presbyterians to that area after 1603. Economic discrimination against Irish linen and beef in the reign of William III after 1689 brought about the migration of about two hundred thousand of these people, between 1710 and 1750 especially to the Shenandoah Valley and to the Ohio Valley in Pennsylvania.

From Continental Europe

The control of the medieval universal church in Europe gave way even earlier than in England to national or state churches holding to the principles of the Reformation. In addition, the Anabaptists, who did not accept the state church principle, held to the major theological emphases of the reformers. Both these groups provided migrants to the New World.

The *Lutherans* of Germany and Scandinavia derived their church from the efforts of Martin Luther (1483-1546). Luther was the son of peasant parents who became prosperous through the ownership of mines and smelters. His father wanted him to study law after he graduated from Erfurt with his B.A. and M.A. in scholastic philosophy, but Luther, after a frightening experience in a thunderstorm, entered a monastery, where he worked zealously to achieve merit with God. After he received his doctorate in theology, he began to lecture in theology at the new university of Wittenberg. Preparation for his lectures by the close study of the Psalms, Romans and Galatians led him into an experience of justification by faith alone. This doctrine and the assertion of the priesthood of believers, coupled with the viewpoint that the Bible rather than the church was the sole authority, led him to attack the claims of the Roman Catholic church. This church claimed a monopoly on salvation, which could be received only through the sacraments dispensed by the hierarchy.

Printed tracts of 1520 spread Luther's doctrines all over Germany after his initial attack on the abuse of indulgences in his Ninety-five Theses in 1517. Debates, then an appearance before the Diet, an assembly of the princes of the Holy Roman Empire, led to an open break with the church and excommunication. While hiding at Wartburg Castle, Luther began to translate the Bible into German. Supported by Frederick, prince of Saxony, and other Protestant princes, Lutheranism flourished in Germany until it was strong enough to take the field in battle with the imperial forces. The treaty of Augsburg in 1555 granted toleration to Lutherans in Germany.

Nationalism in Sweden, the translation of the Bible into Swedish, and the preaching of Olavus Petri brought the Reformation to that land. Similarly, in Denmark Lutheranism became the faith of the people. Swedish Lutherans were later to settle on the Delaware, and German Lutherans were to come to Pennsylvania.

Switzerland was the home of the *Reformed* or *Presbyterian* wing of the Reformation. Ulrich Zwingli in the northern cities of Zurich and Berne, through his debates with Roman Catholic priests, was able to persuade the democratic city councils to accept Protestantism. After Zwingli's death in battle between Roman Catholic and Protestant cantons, his followers gradually merged their efforts with those of Calvin.

John Calvin laid solid foundations in Geneva in conjunction with his predecessor Farel. His *Institutes of the Christian Religion*, first published in 1536, was the foremost theological work of the era. It built a system of theology on the basis of the sovereignty of God, who unconditionally elects some totally depraved sinners to salvation and leaves others under condemnation. The limited atonement is for the elect, who will be irresistibly won by the Holy Spirit and eternally kept from loss of their salvation. It was this theology which provided the basis for the Puritan thought of New England and for the Reformed and Presbyterian groups. Geneva became a model and refuge for those of like faith and adherents of a polity based upon representative democratic government of the church.

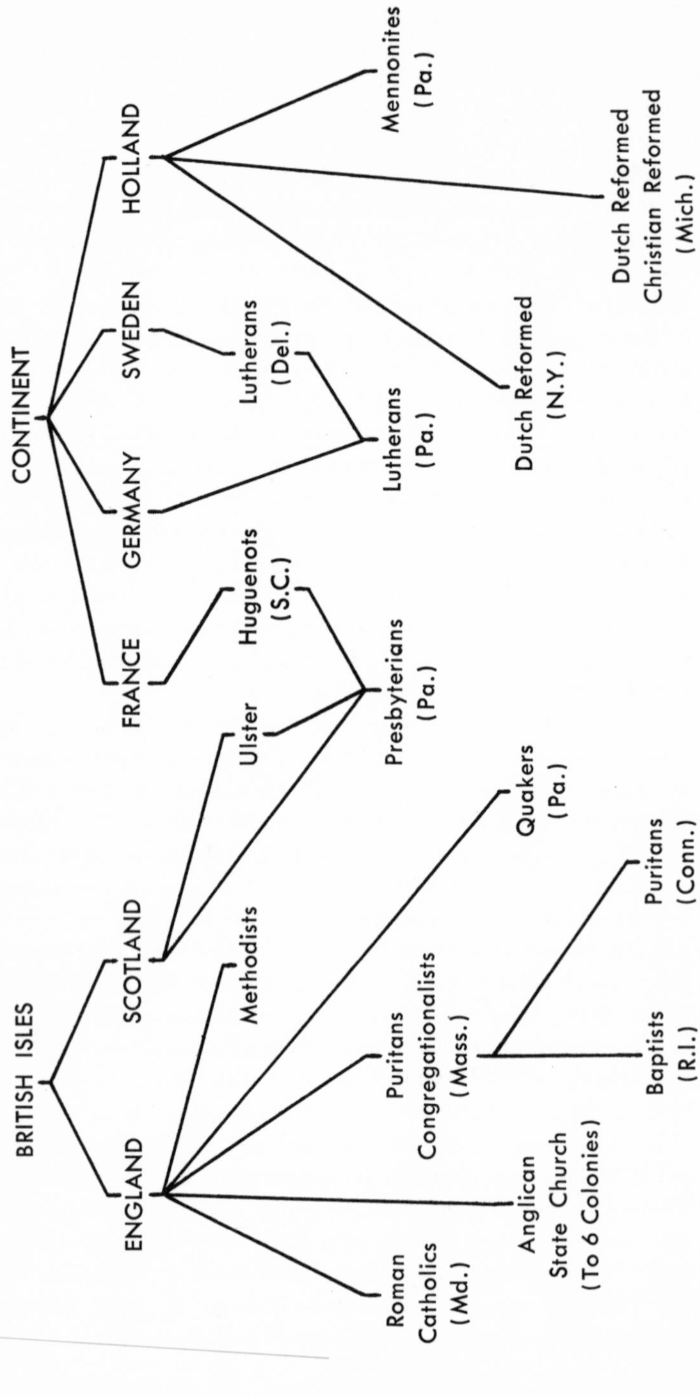

THE HERITAGE OF THE REFORMATION IN THE UNITED STATES

Lutheran ideas, the earlier provision of a French Bible by Lefèvre, and Calvinistic ideas promoted the growth of the Huguenot movement in France, which was organized into a national church in 1559. After the bloody massacre in 1572, in which thousands of Huguenots lost their lives, and ensuing warfare, they were granted toleration by the Edict of Nantes in 1598 until its revocation by Louis XIV in 1685. Many of these Calvinists then fled to the thirteen colonies, particularly South Carolina.

Scotland also, under the leadership of John Knox and in spite of the opposition of the Catholic monarch Mary Stuart, accepted the Reformation by 1560 and ended her traditional alliance with France. Knox provided creed, discipline and a prayer book for the church. The system of representative session, presbytery, synod, and general assembly in Scotland was imported directly to the thirteen colonies by Scottish migrants from Scotland and indirectly from northern Ireland by the Scottish settlers from Ulster. Some Scottish divines between 1643 and 1649 united in the Westminster Assembly with the Presbyterians of England in revolt against Charles I. This assembly provided the later American Presbyterian churches with the Westminster Confession and the Longer and Shorter Catechisms.

The struggle to create a Reformed state church in Holland was linked with the struggle for independence from Spain. By 1581 the Dutch declared their independence. This was finally recognized by Spain in 1648. Dutch Reformed settlers came to New Amsterdam (New York) to engage in trade, and thus provided the early Dutch Reformed element of our population.

The *Anabaptists* rejected the state church in favor of one completely divorced from the state and made up of adult, regenerated, baptized believers. They took the Bible, to be literally interpreted, as their standard for faith and conduct. Many of them were pacifists, some communistic, and many refused to take oaths or do military service. This group originated with Conrad Grebel, who broke with Zwingli over infant baptism. When persecuted for their stand, some fled to Austria and others to the Netherlands, where a converted Roman Catholic priest, Menno Simons, organized them into the Mennonite church. It was some of these Mennonites who provided the first settlers of Germantown in Pennsylvania. Although fanatics, such as the communistic polygamous followers of John of Leyden, brought discredit upon the name Anabaptist, this movement

appealed to the workers and peasants in a way the middle class
Lutheran, Reformed and Anglican movements could not.

Such were the British and European antecedents of Christianity in the American colonies. This heritage can still be dis-
cerned in American religious thought, life and polity.

BIBLIOGRAPHY

OLMSTEAD. *HRUS*. Pp. 1-24.
SWEET. *SRA*. Pp. 8-25.

Bibliography for Era from 1607 to 1865

Sources:

SWEET, WILLIAM W. (ed.). *Religion on the American Frontier, 1783-
1850*. 4 vols. Chicago: University of Chicago Press, 1931-1946.
Collections of documents concerning the Methodist, Presbyterian,
Baptist and Congregational churches on the frontier.

Histories:

BATES, ERNEST S. *American Faith* . . . New York: W. W. Norton and
Co., Inc., 1940. An account of American religious history to 1865
which emphasizes the economic factor and class division as the
main keys to understanding American religious history.
STEPHENSON, GEORGE M. *The Puritan Heritage*. New York: The
Macmillan Co., 1952. A good survey of American religious life to
1865.
SWEET, WILLIAM W. *Religion in Colonial America*. New York: Charles
Scribner's Sons, 1942. A scholarly detailed survey of religious life
in the colonial era.
————. *Religion in the Development of American Culture, 1765-1840*.
New York: Charles Scribner's Sons, 1952.

2

THE ANGLICAN ESTABLISHED CHURCHES IN THE THIRTEEN COLONIES

THE ANGLICAN CHURCH had elements of great strength with its bishop and clergy linked with the early church through the doctrine of apostolic succession, its Book of Common Prayer, and its beliefs summarized in the Thirty-nine Articles. This, combined with support from England, even though there was no American bishop until after the Revolution, gave it a privileged position in the colonies. In six of the thirteen colonies it was established by law during the colonial era.

Early foundations in *Virginia* were laid by the London Company, whose charter from the king in 1606 called for an Anglican establishment. Robert Hunt, Anglican chaplain of the first settlers sent out by the company in 1607, held the first service under the protection of "an old saile" with logs for seats and pulpit. He died after two years, but his place in the communal settlement was taken in 1611 by Alexander Whitaker, a pastor with Puritan leanings. Many of the earliest settlers, who died in great numbers because of malaria contracted by living in the low swampy land, were Puritan Anglicans.

In 1619 the communal organization gave way to private landholdings and to representative government through an elected assembly. "Single young women of blameless reputation" were sent out to be wives of the settlers, and the position of the church was strengthened by provision for the support of the established church. The successful growth of tobacco by John Rolfe in 1612, coupled with the introduction of slavery in 1619, laid the foundation for economic progress. In the first colony, church and state were united. By 1624 the crown took over control and Virginia became a royal colony.

Privilege apparently was no guarantee of vigor, because the

Anglican church remained weak for a long time. There was a lack of trained, able clergy because good men could get better positions in England, and with no bishop or college there were no means to provide clergy from the area. Parishes were too large and the salaries paid in tobacco or corn were too small. The vestries were composed of men who handled both civil and ecclesiastical affairs for the parish. Because a minister installed by the governor would be in the parish indefinitely, the vestry refused to present a man for installation in many cases in order to keep him from gaining full legal control over the parish. After 1632 the churches in the colony were under the absentee control of the Bishop of London, who alone could appoint and send out ministers.

When Henry Compton became bishop in 1675, he decided to send out a commissary to represent him in the colony. James Blair (1656-1743), a graduate of Aberdeen with an M.A. from Edinburgh, became the first commissary to Virginia in 1689. After service as pastor of Bruton Church in Williamsburg, he advocated higher salaries, insisted that churches present their ministers for induction into office in order to give them life tenure, obtained representation for the clergy on the governor's council, and disciplined drunken or immoral clergy. His most important proposal was to found a college to train future ministers. Through his efforts the College of William and Mary was chartered in 1693, and Blair became its first president. Christopher Wren was the architect of its first building. This provision for training ministers and the enlistment of able men from England provided better ministers for the parishes.

Maryland, which had been founded by the Calverts in 1634, had no established church for some time, because the Calverts wished to provide a refuge for persecuted Roman Catholics (who were in the minority) and to build up a prosperous colony. For these reasons toleration was granted to all religious groups except Unitarians and Jews. This principle was enacted into law by the passage of the Toleration Act of 1649 by the assembly. The presence of increasing numbers of Anglicans led to the passage of acts in 1692 and 1696 to establish the Church of England in Maryland, but these were disallowed. Not until 1702 was the third act approved in England, and the Anglican church established in Maryland. The act provided for the choosing of vestrymen and churchwardens to conduct the affairs of the parish.

In 1695 or 1696 Bishop Compton selected Thomas Bray (1656-

1730), an able Anglican clergyman, to become commissary in Maryland. Although Bray spent only a year in the colony, his work in England made a lasting contribution to the success of the church in the colonies. He was able to get money to provide libraries for the clergy and to recruit able men to fill the vacant parishes. In 1698 or 1699 he organized the Society for the Promotion of Christian Knowledge to provide literature for colonial ministers and their people. After a short residence in Maryland in 1700, he returned to England. In 1701 he was able to secure a charter for the Society for the Propagation of the Gospel in Foreign Parts. Between 1702 and 1726 this society sent out about three hundred missionaries and was largely responsible for the network of Anglican churches organized along the Atlantic coast.

While the early charter of *South Carolina* called for public support for the Anglican church, it did permit toleration to dissenters. Several acts were passed to create an established church, but not until 1706 was an act approved. The work of the Society for the Propagation of the Gospel helped to provide good clergy for the colony. An act in 1715 provided for the establishment of the Anglican church in *North Carolina,* but the establishment was never as popular in that colony as in South Carolina because of large numbers of dissenters.

Georgia was founded in 1732 by James Oglethorpe as a haven for those who had been imprisoned for their debts, and religious liberty was granted to all except Roman Catholics. Both the Wesleys and Whitefield served the church in Georgia, and Whitefield founded Bethesda Orphanage at Savannah. After Georgia became a royal colony, the Anglican church was established by law in 1758.

New York was the only colony in the North to have an Anglican establishment. Until 1664, when the English captured the colony from the Dutch, the Dutch Reformed church had been the only recognized church, having been granted recognition by the English. When the pro-Catholic James II fled from England and William and Mary became the rulers in 1689, William instructed Henry Sloughter to work for an established church in the colony. The assembly passed an act in 1693[1] which provided for the settlement and maintenance of ministers in New York City and three counties. The six parishes were to have "a good sufficient Protestant minister" supported by annual taxes. Because this

[1]Peter G. Mode, *Sourcebook and Bibliographical Guide to American Church History* (Menasha, Wis.: George Banta Publishing Co., 1921), p. 138.

was interpreted to mean only Anglican ministers, the act made that church the established church in New York. Trinity Church in 1697 became the first organized Anglican parish in New York.

Anglican churches were organized in other middle and New England colonies, but in none of them did they become strong enough to bring about an establishment. Puritan opposition and what amounted to Puritan state churches in New England, and Quaker opposition in Pennsylvania and New Jersey, prevented such a development.

Connection with the state, especially in the South, seemed to promote spiritual slackness, and it was difficult even with the work of the Society for the Propagation of the Gospel to obtain enough good men to provide the necessary spiritual vitality. The absence of any colonial bishop until after the American Revolution prevented effective on-the-spot leadership necessary for the growth of a dynamic church.

BIBLIOGRAPHY

ADDISON, JAMES T. *The Episcopal Church in the United States, 1789-1931.* New York: Charles Scribner's Sons, 1951.

MANROSS, WILLIAM W. *A History of the American Episcopal Church.* New York: Morehouse-Gorham Co., 1950.

Useful standard histories of American Episcopalianism.

OLMSTEAD. *HRUS.* Pp. 40-61.

SWEET. *SRA.* Pp. 26-43.

THOMPSON, HENRY P. *Thomas Bray.* London: Society for Promoting of Christian Knowledge, 1954.

3

PURITANISM IN NEW ENGLAND

ENGLISH PURITANISM shortly before the great migration from England to what was to become Massachusetts had, under the intellectual leadership of William Ames (1576-1633), adopted the concept that the state church should be a confederation of sovereign local congregations which could call and ordain ministers. Dissent from this type of establishment was not to be tolerated. The Separatists, under the influence of the teachings of Robert Browne (1550-1633), rejected any established church and insisted that regenerate persons in an autonomous local church, bound to one another and to Christ by a church covenant, constituted a church which could choose its own officers. This principle was adopted in the Plymouth colony; but the principle of Ames, in Salem and Boston and finally in all the New England colonies. Puritans, mainly from the yeoman farmer and merchant middle classes of the London and Midlands areas, became settlers in these colonies.

Beginnings in Massachusetts

Plymouth became the site of a Separatist colony in the New World in 1620. A congregation of Separatists fled from Scrooby in Nottinghamshire to Holland in 1608 under the leadership of their pastor, John Robinson. Alarmed lest their children become a part of the Dutch population, they returned to England to migrate to their "New England." Thomas Weston, a London businessman, and his associates raised seven thousand pounds to provide ships and supplies so that they could found a fishing and trading colony. Slightly more than one hundred persons sailed on the "Mayflower" under the spiritual leadership of William Brewster and the later political leader William Bradford. To provide stable government when they landed, the Pilgrims drew up the Mayflower Compact,[1] which was really a church covenant ap-

[1] Peter G. Mode, *Sourcebook and Bibliographical Guide to American Church History* (Menasha, Wis.: George Banta Publishing Co., 1921), p. 49.

plied to a political situation. This was their only legal basis for government until 1691, when Plymouth merged with Massachusetts.

Because their patent was for settlement in Virginia, they had to negotiate with the New England Company for permission to settle on its lands. Only the original landowners and regenerate freemen were granted the right to vote for the governor and the the Council of Assistants. John Lyford, an Anglican clergyman, was sent out to be their minister in 1624, but the colonists expelled him. Not until the arrival of Ralph Smith in 1629 and Roger Williams in 1631 did they have a minister to administer the sacraments, although Brewster had provided earlier spiritual leadership. Several leaders, such as Bradford, Standish and Alden, led in the agreement to pay their London partners eighteen hundred pounds in nine annual installments and to take over six hundred pounds due to the company's creditors. The colony soon became independent. By 1630 the colony numbered three hundred, and regular growth continued because of their more tolerant spirit.

A small group of businessmen in Dorchester, England had founded a fishing colony at Gloucester, but it failed. John White, the Puritan minister in Dorchester, became interested in a venture for settlement. A land grant was obtained from the Council of New England, and John Endicott was sent out with sixty people in 1628 to what became *Salem*. In 1629 two Puritan ministers, Samuel Skelton and Francis Higginson, came and were reordained by the congregation to become teachers of the church. This heritage of Puritan Congregationalism which the Salem settlers brought with them, rather than the kindly medical ministrations during the first hard winter by Dr. Samuel Fuller, a deacon of the Plymouth church, accounts for their congregational system. They still felt that they were a congregation in the state church though they rejected episcopacy.[2]

Charles I had granted a charter for a Massachusetts Bay Company to Puritans of East Anglia in 1629, and in 1630, under the leadership of John Winthrop, about a thousand Puritans, bringing their charter, came and created settlements at *Boston* and other towns. Between 1629 and 1639, when Charles ruled without a Parliament, about twenty thousand Puritans came to New England. The first General Court in 1631 linked the franchise with church membership by limiting it to regenerate church members, thus creating a practical union of church and state. The church

[2]*Ibid.*, pp. 62-65.

was also supported by public taxes. By 1636 the General Court
gave power over the church to the magistrates and, later, control as to who preached what and where. The clergy, through
control of the franchise by choice of church members, the preaching of election day sermons, and the giving of advice to magistrates on public matters, had much to do with government, although technically New England did not have a theocracy. The
General Court made up of the governor and freemen had full
legal authority.

The Swarming of the Puritans

Rhode Island owes its existence to the rigid Puritan policies
which forced more independent souls to move to other areas.
Roger Williams (ca. 1603-1683) had demonstrated Separatist
tendencies early in his ministry. His good work as a shorthand
clerk in the court brought him to the attention of the great English
jurist Edward Coke, who made it possible for him to get college
preparatory training and who helped him to go to Cambridge,
where he earned his B.A. Possibly because of his Separatist
tendencies he did not receive his M.A. He married Mary Barnard,
a maid in the Masham home, where he was chaplain.

Williams' radical Separatist tendencies led to his migration in
1631 to Boston, where he was called to be a teacher, but he
refused to settle either there or at Salem because he believed
that the congregation was "unseparated" from Anglicanism and
asserted that the magistrate had no power in spiritual matters.
He went to Plymouth, where he made his living for two years by
assisting the minister, Ralph Smith, and by farming and trading
with the Indians. In 1635, after Samuel Skelton's death, Williams
came back to Salem as a teacher, but got into trouble by his
assertion that the colonists should not take Indian land except
by treaty and payment. His desire to separate civil authority from
spiritual authority finally led to a sentence of banishment by the
General Court in 1635. When the magistrates decided to return
him to England by force, he fled in the winter of 1636 to the
present area of Providence, where by treaty and purchase he obtained land from the Indians. Before the end of 1636 he was
joined by more than thirty others and set up a colony.

Anne Hutchinson and her followers later were driven out of
Massachusetts Bay and in 1638 settled at Newport and Ports-
mouth. She believed that the covenant of works had been super-
seded by the covenant of grace and that the Holy Spirit indwelt

and illuminated the believer. The latter position in her interpretation was close to an inner light doctrine. At meetings in her house, where the previous Sunday sermon was discussed, she stated that only her brother-in-law, John Wheelwright, and John Cotton, who had been her minister in England, preached the covenant of grace. She was banished by the civil authorities and expelled in the winter of 1638 shortly before the birth of her child.

Samuel Gorton and his followers were forced out of the Massachusetts Bay Colony for teaching inner illumination by the Holy Spirit and the desirability of separation of church and state. He founded Warwick in what became Rhode Island. Thus these forced migrations from Puritan settlements were the occasion for the founding of Rhode Island.

A voluntary swarming of the Puritans under the leadership of Thomas Hooker (1586-1647) resulted in the founding of *Connecticut*. Traders, such as Edward Winslow and John Oldham, reported the presence of much fertile land in the Connecticut River valley. Hooker and his followers, who were more democratic than the Bay Puritans, requested permission to go to this area. By 1636 they settled Wethersfield and later Hartford and Windsor. In 1639 they adopted the "Fundamental Orders of Connecticut." Church membership was not made a condition for exercise of the franchise as in the Bay Colony. Property holders of good character were allowed to vote.

In the meantime in 1638 New Haven had been founded as a Bible commonwealth by the Rev. John Davenport and a merchant friend, Theophilus Eaton. In 1639 they set up a government with the suffrage restricted to church members. In 1662 the Bible commonwealth and the Connecticut settlements were united to form the colony of Connecticut.

Attempts to colonize the area which became *New Hampshire* were made in the 1620's by Fernando Gorges and John Mason. It fell under the control of the Bay Colony, but in 1679 New Hampshire became a separate Puritan colony. Refugees as well as settlers from the Bay Colony brought about Puritan control.

Development of Puritanism

Puritan theology in New England was Calvinistic but somewhat modified by the ideas of the Cambridge Platonists. They had been influenced by Peter Ramus (1515-1572), who had rejected Aristotle in favor of Platonic ideas. Basing all his theology on the Bible, this Puritan asserted the sovereignty of God and the total depravity of man through Adam, the federal head of the race, who broke the covenant between God and himself. Because this covenant of works with Adam failed, God graciously set up the new covenant of grace in Christ, by which the elect were chosen and irresistibly brought to salvation by the Holy Spirit, who applied the work of the atonement, limited to the elect, to their hearts. They believed that the elect ones were also united by a covenant to God and to one another in a church of regenerate believers, who alone could elect magistrates and church leaders. This system of thought led to a rigid code of ethics. The covenant concept was carried over into political life in such documents as the Mayflower Compact.

Worship was carried on in the severely plain New England meetinghouse. Later, steeples fashioned after the pattern of those built by Wren were added. Plain, high square pews filled the room. Psalm singing, Bible reading, prayers and an hour-long sermon were important parts of the service in these churches. The Bay Psalm Book (1640) was the first book to be printed in America.

The Cambridge Synod was called by the General Court in 1646 to consider matters of theology and polity. It consisted of representatives of the New England churches. In its final meeting in 1648 the synod adopted the Calvinistic Westminster Confession, which had been prepared by the English and Scottish divines of the Westminster Assembly in England. This action was approved later by the General Court. Another synod in 1680 adopted the Calvinistic English Congregational Savoy Declaration of 1658.

The Cambridge Synod gave even more attention to matters of polity. John Cotton, Richard Mather and Ralph Partridge were delegated as a committee to prepare a statement on church government. The synod meeting in September, 1648, adopted the statement which was known as the Cambridge Platform.[3] It emphasized the church of believers united to God and to each other by a church covenant. Its officers, pastors, teachers, elders and deacons were to be selected by the people. Ministers were to be called and ordained by the local congregation. The autonomy of the local church was asserted, but churches were exhorted to be of mutual aid to each other.

In the South, education was mainly a private matter of tutors or a few families hiring a teacher, but in Puritan New England

[3]*Ibid.*, pp. 76, 77.

it was linked with public action by the General Court. The "old deluder Satan" Act of 1647 provided that every township of fifty families had to set up an elementary school supported by fees or by public funds. Similar action was taken in Connecticut in 1650. All the textbooks—and often the Bible was the sole textbook—were religious or ethical in content.

Secondary schools were private and mainly concerned with preparing the child for college. A Latin school was set up in Boston in 1635 with Ezekiel Cheever as its master. Massachusetts Bay provided by law in 1647 that each town of one hundred families should set up a grammar school to fit "ye youths" for "ye university" (Harvard), and other towns followed suit. Study of the classical languages was a major part of the curriculum.

Colleges were founded to provide godly leadership in church and state. The pamphlet *New England's First Fruits* (1643) stated that the college (Harvard) was established "to advance learning" in order to provide a trained ministry.[4] Harvard was founded in 1636 to meet this need as the result of a grant from the General Court. This was augmented in 1638 by John Harvard's will, which left half of his estate and his books to the college, which was then given his name. Henry Dunster, president from 1640 to 1654 when he became a Baptist, graduated his first class of nine in 1642. Yale was founded in 1701 for similar purposes.[5]

Although preoccupied with theology and church government, the Puritans did not completely neglect the Indians. John Eliot (1604-1690), a graduate of Cambridge, who was teacher and later pastor of the Roxbury church for nearly sixty years, became interested in the Indians and learned their language. He began work among them in 1646 and by 1663 had translated the Bible into their language. This was the first Bible printed in the thirteen colonies. He gathered his converts into self-governing towns of Christian Indians, such as Natick. He had about 3,000 in over thirty villages by 1674, but his work was undone when many of these towns were destroyed and the converts killed or scattered in King Philip's War in 1675. Not content with his pastoral and missionary work, Eliot was also the founder of Roxbury Latin School. The Mayhew family also carried on missionary work among the Indians of Martha's Vineyard for several generations.

John Cotton (1584-1652) was a leader in the development of Puritan thought. He entered Trinity College at Cambridge at

[4]*Ibid.*, pp. 73-75.
[5]*Ibid.*, pp. 109, 110.

the age of thirteen, and became vicar of St. Botolph's Church in Boston, England, after his ordination in 1612. Because of the Laudian persecution, he migrated to the colonies in 1633. Here he became teacher of the First Church in Boston. Cotton wrote *The Keys of the Kingdom of Heaven* in 1644 and *The Way of the Churches of Christ in New England* in 1645. He also helped to formulate the pattern of government and the theological Cambridge Platform of 1648, which set the later theological and governmental pattern of the churches of New England. His opposition finally drove Roger Williams and Anne Hutchinson out of the colony, and was one reason for the voluntary migration of Thomas Hooker and his followers.

Increase Mather (1639-1723) was of similar stature in the second generation of Puritan leaders. He received his A.B. degree from Harvard at the age of seventeen and earned his A.M. degree at Trinity College in Ireland. In 1664 he became teacher in the Second Church of Boston and served as president of Harvard between 1685 and 1701. His son, Cotton Mather, wrote *Magnalia Christi Americana*, which is the foremost work of church history in colonial America.

The Decline of Puritanism

The Half-Way Covenant of 1662[6] marked an important step in the theological dilution of Puritanism. Ideally the church was made up of regenerate believers and their children, who through their parents were members of the covenant. Many of these children of the often unconverted second generation had no conversion experience. Should their children be admitted to the Lord's Supper and be baptized? Because the franchise was linked with church membership, this was an important question. A General Synod of all the Massachusetts churches was called, and this synod in 1662 adopted the Half-Way Covenant. This allowed second generation unregenerate parents to present their third generation children for baptism, but these children could not participate in communion nor vote in church elections unless they owned the covenant for themselves and became church members upon profession of faith.

This principle of providing religious services to the unregenerate was extended still further in 1677 by Solomon Stoddard,[7]

[6]*Ibid.*, pp. 83-85.
[7]H. Shelton Smith, Robert T. Handy, and Lefferts A. Loetscher, *American Christianity; An Historical Interpretation with Representative Documents* (New York: Charles Scribner's Sons, 1960), pp. 219-224.

the grandfather of Jonathan Edwards and the pastor at North-ampton. He permitted unregenerate members of the church to take part in the communion service because it might be a means whereby they would become converted.

Puritanism received still another blow with the witchcraft trials and execution in 1692, of more than twenty "witches" at Salem and several others in other areas. Samuel Sewall's diary describes this episode in mass hysteria. The incident began with accusa-tions of witchcraft by three children all under thirteen years of age. Later, several of those involved publicly repented of their part in the incident.

"Liberal" tendencies in organization and liturgy also caused difficulties. The Brattle Street Church, the fourth Congregational church in Boston, was organized in 1699 on the basis that any child could have baptism, thus separating membership from con-version. It brought the Lord's Prayer into the church service and the reading of Scripture without comment ("dumb reading"). Any contributor could also help to select the minister.

The Massachusetts Proposals of 1705 provided for the organiza-tion of ministerial associations which would examine and license ministers. Churches without a minister were to seek the advice of the association before calling a pastor. The proposal to have a standing council of pastors and laymen in each association to supervise the churches and make binding decisions was not ac-cepted, although the other proposals were adopted. These pro-posals were opposed by John Wise (1652-1725), who favored the earlier more democratic government in church and state.

In Connecticut the Saybrook Platform of 1708[8] was a similar step in the direction of Presbyterianism. The Savoy Declara-tion was adopted as a theological standard, and consociations of representatives of churches with power over each local group were agreed upon, as well as ministerial associations with power to ordain and advise ministerial candidates. The government of Connecticut adopted this semi-Presbyterian plan.

The Puritan clergy called for reform, but the dilution of church membership by the Half-Way Covenant and the centralizing of authority under the Saybrook Platform did not halt but rather stimulated the decline of religion. With decline of religion came decline of ethics. The Great Awakening of the seventeenth cen-tury arrested this decline for a time, but in later years many of the New England churches drifted into Unitarianism.

While many would criticize the Puritans, one should not mini-

8Mode, *op. cit., pp.* 105-108.

mize their influence upon American culture. Our system of representative and responsible democracy at least indirectly owes much to their inspiration. State governments in New England were given a religious sanction. The American tendencies to thrift and demand for morality still owe something to the Puritan code of life. Congregationalist denominations are still another heritage of Puritanism.

BIBLIOGRAPHY

ATKINS, GAIUS G., and FAGLEY, FREDERICK L. *History of American Congregationalism*. Boston: Pilgrim Press, 1942. A scholarly history of American Congregationalism.

BALTIS, EMERY. *Saint and Sectaries*. Chapel Hill, N.C.: University of North Carolina, 1962. Useful biography of Anne Hutchinson.

KITTREDGE, GEORGE L. *Witchcraft in Old and New England*. Cambridge: Harvard University Press, 1929. A scholarly standard account.

MILLER, PERRY. *Orthodoxy in Massachusetts, 1630-1650*. Cambridge: Harvard University Press, 1933. Contention that the Puritans of Salem and Boston were non-Separatist Anglicans who came to reform the Church of England but became Congregationalists in America.

OLMSTEAD. *HRUS*. Pp. 62-90.

SIMPSON, ALAN. *Puritanism in Old and New England*. Chicago: University of Chicago Press, 1955.

SWEET. *SRA*. Pp. 44-65, 155-159.

UPHAM, CHARLES W. *Salem Witchcraft* . . . 2 vols. Boston: Wiggin and Lunt, 1867. Much source material in Volume 2.

WERTENBAKER, THOMAS J. *The Puritan Oligarchy*. New York: Charles Scribner's Sons, 1947. See also bibliography in Chapter 4 for biographies of Roger Williams.

4

COLONIAL EXPERIMENTS IN FREEDOM OF RELIGION

WHILE THE PURITANS adopted a form of democracy in New England, the linking of the franchise with church membership, except in Connecticut, created a union of church and state which had no provision for freedom of conscience. Baptists and Quakers were persecuted for their faith by whippings, banishment, and even by hanging in the case of some Quakers. Separation of church and state and freedom of conscience were left to the leaders in Maryland, Rhode Island and Pennsylvania to develop. Religious heterogeneity and pluralism in these colonies replaced the homogeneity of the southern and New England colonies.

Maryland and Religious Toleration

Relatively few Roman Catholics came to the English colonies, although large numbers settled in Canada as fur trappers or traders. Others explored parts of North America for France or Spain. Priests of the Franciscan order particularly took up the responsibility of converting the Indians in the new lands discovered by French and Spanish explorers. The lack of toleration for Roman Catholics in England made it difficult for them to take part in colonization except in the reign of the Roman Catholic James II. Moreover, many of them were of the landed gentry, and as long as they kept their religion secret, they had little incentive to leave their possessions in England to go to English colonies where, except for Maryland, they would have no more toleration.

Apart from Maryland, Roman Catholic influence in the United States at that time was limited to Indian missions in the West. Spanish Franciscan friars established a chain of missions along the California coast in the eighteenth century to convert and civilize the Indians in those areas. There is also a legacy of early

Roman Catholicism in Louisiana from the settlement of the French Acadians from Nova Scotia in the mid-eighteenth century.

George Calvert, the first Lord Baltimore (ca. 1580-1632), after his conversion to Roman Catholicism became interested in forming a colony where persecuted Roman Catholics could find a refuge. The king gave him a charter and a grant of land in 1632, but he died before he could make use of it. His son Cecil Calvert (1605-1675) founded Maryland. He decided on religious toleration for all except Jews and Unitarians, and so instructed his first governor. He knew that England would not permit him to found a Roman Catholic colony, and if he could have done so, he would not have been able to realize much profit from it since too few Roman Catholics would have come. Religious toleration would also bring Protestant settlers.

More than two hundred sailed to Maryland and one hundred twenty-eight of them took the oath denying papal authority. About sixteen families and two Jesuit priests were Roman Catholic in this group that founded the colony in 1634. In 1649 Calvert appointed a Protestant governor, who had the local assembly pass a toleration act[1] that gave religious freedom to all except Jews and Unitarians. Earlier, in 1636, he had required all the governors to promise they would trouble no one who believed in Christ. Because the Protestant Anglicans increased in numbers faster than the Romans Catholics, they demanded the establishment of the Anglican church. This was finally approved by the English government in 1702, and Maryland's experiment in limited religious freedom was ended.

The Baptists in Rhode Island

The southern and New England colonies set up churches which had a definite creed, were state churches in a union of church and state, and upheld infant baptism as the way of entrance into the church. Religious groups in the middle colonies might be designated as sect groups. Initially they stressed life rather than doctrine. They looked upon the church as an organism of believers. Such was the case with the groups in Rhode Island, Pennsylvania and, for a time, New Jersey. Many of the immigrants were of lower class persecuted groups, such as the Germans and some of the Scotch-Irish who settled in Pennsylvania. Pioneering stimulated individualism, and the Great Awakening helped to break down denominational barriers. Re-

[1]H. Shelton Smith *et al, American Christianity* (New York: Charles Scribner's Sons, 1960), I, 35-39.

ligion in these colonies displayed the heterogeneity and pluralism that are so characteristic of the American scene.

The roots of the Rhode Island colony are to be found in the swarming of the Puritans from Massachusetts Bay under the leadership of Roger Williams, Anne Hutchinson, Samuel Gorton and John Clarke. Williams developed the basic principles of separation of church and state, freedom of conscience, and the necessity of treaty and purchase of land as the only fair way of dealing with the Indians. With others he helped to establish the Baptistic principle of adult believer baptism. This emphasis was more important than whether or not baptism was by affusion or immersion, because the basic principles stated above flow from it. In addition, he laid the early foundation in Rhode Island of government by contract or consent of the people.

Convinced of the necessity of adult believer baptism, Williams was baptized, most likely by affusion, in the spring of 1639 by Ezekiel Holliman, and then he baptized Holliman and several others. Williams did not remain with the group very long but withdrew to become a "Seeker" even though he was closer to the Baptists than to any other group. John Clarke (1609-1676) had also organized a church at Newport as early as 1638, but until 1648 there are no clear-cut records indicating that it was a Baptist church. Thus it is still a matter of question as to whether the Providence or the Newport church has the honor of being the first Baptist church in the United States.

Once established in Rhode Island, the Baptist movement soon spread to other colonies in the face of severe persecution. John Clarke, Obadiah Holmes and John Crandall traveled in 1651 at the request of William Winter to worship with him in his home near Lynn in the Bay Colony. They were taken by the police, imprisoned, tried and sentenced to fines or flogging. Clarke and Crandall were freed, as someone paid their fines. But Holmes refused to permit this in his case, and was given thirty lashes.[2]

The Baptist principles even enlisted Henry Dunster, the president of Harvard. His conviction that baptism of adult believers was scriptural led him in 1653 to fail to present his fourth child for baptism. In the fall of 1654 he disturbed a service in Cambridge to set forth his position on baptism. His resignation as president was accepted, and subsequently he was admonished by the General Court. By 1663 the first Baptist church in the Bay

[2]Peter G. Mode, *Sourcebook and Bibliographical Guide to American Church History* (Menasha, Wis.: George Banta Publishing Co., 1921), pp. 283-285.

Colony was founded at Rehoboth under the leadership of John Myles.

Growth of the Baptists was even greater in the middle and southern colonies during and after the Great Awakening. The first Baptist association of five churches was created in 1707, and in 1742 it adopted a strong Calvinistic confession. From this point on, the future was to be more with Calvinistic than Arminian Baptists. All, like Roger Williams, stood for separation of church and state and freedom of conscience, which removed religious affairs from civil control and democracy.

Even though he became a Seeker, Williams still served the colonists of Rhode Island well until his death in 1683. In 1643 he went to England to prevent Massachusetts from taking over the colony and to secure a charter. This he obtained in 1644. While in England he wrote *The Bloudy Tenent of Persecution for Cause of Conscience*, which upheld separation of church and state and freedom of conscience against the contrary view in a pamphlet by John Cotton.[3] On his return to Rhode Island, Williams succeeded in getting the towns to unite under the charter, and he was elected chief magistrate of Rhode Island from 1644 to 1647. In 1651 he and John Clarke went to England to get the charter of 1644 confirmed. While there he wrote *The Bloudy Tenent Yet More Bloudy* in his pamphlet war with Cotton. By 1663 the desired charter was secured. Williams became president of the new government between 1654 and 1657 and promoted his basic principles of democracy, separation of church and state, and religious freedom. His services to the cause of freedom in the thirteen colonies were great, and his principles are still upheld by the Baptists.

The Quakers

Quaker principles were initially planted in the thirteen colonies by Quaker missionary zeal rather than by migration, even though later Pennsylvania and, for a time, New Jersey were Quaker colonies. Mary Fisher and Ann Austin came to Boston to preach in 1656, but were deported as were others at a later date. The General Court of Massachusetts in 1656 decreed whipping and hard labor followed by banishment for Quakers. Between 1659 and 1661 four Quakers, one of whom was Mary Dyer, were executed for their faith. Persecution in New England ceased by 1677. While Quakers were not persecuted in Rhode Island, Roger Williams opposed their ideas in word and pamphlet and even

[3]Smith, *op. cit.*, I, 151-158.

debated publicly with some of them. Except in Rhode Island and
the Carolinas they were persecuted, but the group grew either
in spite of or because of persecution. The first monthly meetings
in America came into being before 1660. A visit by George Fox
in 1672 and 1673 helped to stimulate the rise of Quakerism.

More extensive settlement took place in New Jersey. Shortly
after 1664 James, Duke of York, gave the area to his friends
Berkeley and Carteret. Berkeley's share was bought by Quakers
John Fenwick and Edward Byllinge in 1674. Out of it they
formed West Jersey. The initial agreement of 1677 provided
for democratic government and freedom of religion. The Quakers
also obtained control of East Jersey after Carteret's death in 1679,
and Robert Barclay, the Quaker theologian, was made governor.
By 1692 Quaker ownership gave way to Anglican stockholders,
and New Jersey became a royal province ten years later.

Temporary Quaker control in New Jersey was replaced by
Quaker ownership and settlement in Pennsylvania through the
efforts of William Penn (1644-1718), who had been interested
in the experiment in New Jersey. Penn, the son of an Anglican
admiral, was inclined to Quakerism from his youth and became
a convert in 1667. Charles II, who owed Penn's father sixteen
thousand pounds, gave Penn a grant in Pennsylvania in 1681.
Penn's *Frame of Government* in 1682 upheld both civil and religious liberty in the new colony, and Penn promised settlers land
at forty shillings for a hundred acres. Penn also treated the
Indians fairly by purchasing needed land or securing it by treaty.

Because he widely advertised these principles and offered the
repressed and persecuted a place in Pennsylvania, it became
the home of many groups in addition to the Quakers. By 1690
the population of Pennsylvania was nearly twelve thousand, with
two thousand of these people arriving by 1682.

But, like the Puritans, the Quakers soon suffered a decline
in the high standards of devotion and martyrdom with which the
American colony began. The London yearly meeting of 1737
stated that if the parents were members of a monthly meeting,
their children would be considered members by birthright. This
principle of birthright membership was similar to the Puritan
Half-Way Covenant and, in like fashion, led to spiritual decline.
The necessity of a conversion experience was minimized. Thrift
also led to increase in wealth which brought the temptation
to ostentatious living.

The Quakers showed an early interest in social reform and

were the leaders in England and America in the attempt to ameliorate and then to end slavery. John Woolman (1720-1772) gave the greater part of his life to persuading Quakers to free their slaves. His efforts are recorded in his *Journal*. Anthony Benezet, a Huguenot turned Quaker, wrote books against slavery. It was one of his books which was instrumental in awakening Wesley to the evils of slavery.

Thus did the Baptists of Rhode Island, the Quakers of Pennsylvania and, to a more limited extent, the proprietors of Maryland promote and practice separation of church and state and freedom of religion. After the Revolutionary War, these principles were adopted by the new nation.

BIBLIOGRAPHY

OLMSTEAD. *HRUS*. Pp. 25-39, 91-117.
SWEET. *SRA*. Pp. 66-82, 94-101.

Roman Catholicism:

ELLIS, JOHN T. *American Catholicism*. Chicago: University of Chicago Press, 1956.
MAYNARD, THEODORE. *The Story of American Catholicism*. New York: The Macmillan Co., 1941. Able surveys of the history of American Roman Catholicism.

Baptists:

BROCKUNIER, SAMUEL H. *The Irrepressible Democrat, Roger Williams*. New York: Ronald Press Co., 1940. An able factual biography.
MILLER, PERRY. *Roger Williams: His Contribution to the American Tradition*. Indianapolis: Bobbs-Merrill Co., 1953.
TORBERT, ROBERT G. *A History of the Baptists*. Philadelphia: The Judson Press, 1950. Scholarly account of Baptist history.
WINSLOW, OLA E. *Master Roger Williams, A Biography*. New York: The Macmillan Co., 1957.

Quakers:

BARCLAY, ROBERT. *An Apology for the True Christian Divinity*. London: J. Phillips, 1780.
FOX, GEORGE. *Journal*. Cambridge: Cambridge University Press, 1952.
JONES, RUFUS M., *et al*. *The Quakers in the American Colonies*. London: The Macmillan Co., Ltd., 1923. Detailed account of American Quakerism.
RUSSELL, ELBERT. *The History of Quakerism*. New York: The Macmillan Co., 1942.
WOOLMAN, JOHN. *Journal*. Philadelphia: Friends' Bookstore, 1854.

5

RELIGIOUS PLURALISM IN THE MIDDLE COLONIES

UP TO THE END of the seventeenth century, except for the Swedish and the Dutch, migration to the thirteen colonies was mainly from England. After 1680 an increasing tide of Huguenot, Mennonite, Moravian and other small German groups migrated principally to the middle colonies. Some were members of the major churches of the Reformation and others were of small separatist groups which held to the idea of a pure church made up of converted adults. The more conservative Protestant or Roman Catholic churches drove these latter out.

Churches of the Reformation

Lutheranism had its beginnings in this country among the Swedish settlements along the Delaware. The Dutchman William Usselinx, who served Gustavus Adolphus, promoted a Swedish trading company which was chartered in 1626. Land was bought from the Indians and Fort Christina (Wilmington) was founded in 1638 with fifty settlers under the leadership of Peter Minuit. Soon there were about seven hundred settlers. The Rev. Reorus Torkillus, who arrived in 1639, became the first Lutheran minister in America. When he died, his successor, John Campanius, ministered to the Indians as well as to the settlers. Two of the early Swedish churches, Old Swedes Church in Wilmington, Delaware and Gloria Dei Church in Philadelphia, still memorialize these early Lutheran settlers.

The Swedish colony was taken over by the Dutch in 1655 and both in turn by the English in 1664. Lutheran ministers were permitted to minister to their people under Dutch and English domination, but eventually most of these Swedish settlers joined with the Anglican church.

German Lutherans were the largest group of German migrants during the colonial era. About sixty thousand had settled in

Pennsylvania by 1750 as a result of Penn's liberal and well-advertised policy and an attempt to better their wretched economic conditions in their former European homes. They were too poor usually to bring ministers and pastors with them. Others settled in Maryland, Virginia and North Carolina. Lutherans in Georgia came from Austrian Salzburg in 1731 because of persecution by the Roman Catholic majority. Between 1731 and 1741 about twelve hundred settled in Ebenezer, Georgia.

Most of these Germans kept up contact with the leadership at Halle, a Pietist university in Germany. Henry M. Muhlenberg (1711-1787) was hurriedly sent over in 1742, when the Lutherans of Halle learned that Zinzendorf was trying to unite all Germans in America into one church. Muhlenberg, a graduate of the University of Göttingen, had taught at the Halle orphanage. His motto was *Ecclesia plantanda* ("The church must be planted"). He became pastor of three congregations in and around Philadelphia. In 1745, three aides were sent from Halle with money to build churches. Muhlenberg finally undertook to unify all Lutheran congregations. A synod of six pastors and twenty-four laymen, who represented ten churches, known as the United Pastors then and the Ministerium of Pennsylvania now, was founded in 1748. Uniformity of liturgy, creed and organization was emphasized. From this synod was to emerge after the Revolution the most important of the American Lutheran churches. Muhlenberg also undertook the training of ministers in his own home, and his three sons were among the most notable of his pupils.

The *Reformed* or *Presbyterian* churches in America owe their existence to Puritan settlers from England and Reformed or Presbyterian settlers from Holland, Germany, France, Scotland and Ireland. The earliest of these groups was the Dutch Reformed of New Netherlands. This was a trading colony founded by the Dutch West India Company in 1623 with forts at the present Camden, New Jersey, Albany, New York and, after purchase of Manhattan Island from the Indians in 1624, New Amsterdam, or the present New York City. Because the fur trade was their main interest, and the larger number needed to trade with their Far Eastern colonies, the Dutch migrating to the new colony did not exceed seven thousand. This interest also led to the neglect of religion and education.

Two comforters of the sick were sent over in 1626, and in 1628 Jonas Michaelius, a Dutch Reformed minister who was sent by the classis of Amsterdam, arrived. He served the settlers, but after trying to help the Indians despaired of their conversion.[1] He was replaced in 1633 by Everardus Bogardus, who became economically independent after his marriage in 1638 to a rich widow who owned a sixty-two acre farm on Manhattan. Bogardus clashed with the secular-minded governor, who was able to have a church built by public subscription.

A system of patroonship was set up in 1629, whereby a patroon was given a large tract of land if he would bring over fifty settlers, a minister and a schoolmaster. Patroon Killian Van Rensselaer brought in Johannes Megapolensis, who preached to the heavy-drinking Dutch and even to the Indians until his death in 1670. Desire for wealth and carelessness concerning the welfare of the colonists on the part of the directors of the company created many hardships until Peter Stuyvesant became governor in 1647. But gradually Stuyvesant became intolerant of Lutherans and Friends who settled in the colony.

With the capture of the colony by the English in 1664 Dutch authority came to an end, but the English granted freedom of religion to the six Dutch ministers and thirteen congregations. When James II fled from England, the new governor Sloughter sought to establish the Anglican church. This was done by the Ministry Act of 1693,[2] which provided that there should be a minister in each town of forty families in three counties and New York City. Thus was the Anglican church established in New York. Trinity Church (Anglican) was given a charter in 1697. But the Dutch Reformed church in New York was also granted a charter in 1696. Thus did the Dutch Reformed church in America develop. Later, immigrants from Holland located in Michigan and Iowa, where the Reformed church remains strong even today.

In areas such as the Palatinate along the Rhine, the Reformed faith had taken root. Several German Reformed congregations migrated to Pennsylvania about 1700. Three German congregations in 1725 asked John Philip Boehm (1683-1749), a schoolmaster, to be their pastor. He was ordained by Dutch Reformed ministers in New York in 1729. This ended the two years of strife between him and Michael Weiss, an ordained minister who came in 1727. Michael Schlatter (1716-1790), who arrived in 1746, organized the German Reformed churches into a synod or coetus

[1] H. Shelton Smith *et al, American Christianity* (New York: Charles Scribner's Sons, 1960), I, 56-59.
[2] *Ibid.,* I, 247-249.

in 1747. The church was Calvinistic in theology and Presbyterian in polity, but it worked harmoniously with the German Lutherans in the area.

The Calvinistic Huguenots of France had been tolerated by the passage of the Edict of Nantes in 1598, until 1685 when Louis XIV in order to achieve his ideal of "one law, one king, one faith" revoked it and began to persecute this important middle-class segment of French society. They fled to Prussia, South Africa, England and the thirteen colonies. Because the Dutch were Reformed in faith, many of these Huguenots settled in New York at such places as New Rochelle. About four thousand had settled in New England by 1700. More went to South Carolina, where they came to number between 10 and 20 percent of the population in the eighteenth century. Paul Revere and Peter Faneuil were Huguenots. In all, possibly fifteen thousand came to America. Most of them finally merged with the Reformed or Presbyterian churches.

The Presbyterians from Scotland and northern Ireland or Ulster in the eighteenth century constituted the largest body of persons with Reformed theology and Presbyterian polity to come to the thirteen colonies. The seventeenth century migration came from English Puritan sources to settle in New England. Connecticut had more Presbyterian congregations than did the other New England colonies.

Among the most notable of the early Presbyterian ministers was William Tennent, Sr. (1673-1745), a graduate of Edinburgh University. He trained many of the leading Presbyterian ministers at the time of the Great Awakening. While Anglicanism was strong in the South and Congregationalism in New England, Presbyterianism was strongest in the middle colonies.

Several Presbyterian churches had been founded in the middle colonies by 1700, but Francis Makemie (1658-1708) laid the foundation of organized Presbyterianism in this land. He came to Maryland in 1683 from Ulster by way of Barbados. After forming several Presbyterian churches in Maryland, he traveled to groups in Virginia and the Carolinas. He obtained other ministers on a trip to England in 1704. By 1706 he organized the first American presbytery in a meeting in Philadelphia, to be followed by the organization of the Synod of Philadelphia in 1716 made up of four presbyteries. Thus the church was partially equipped with organization for expansion when the great mass of Scotch-Irish later began to migrate. The Adopting Act of

1729 bound all ministers and licentiates to acceptance of the Westminster Confession.

Makemie also had a part in the fight for freedom of expression. He preached in New York in 1706 and was arrested by order of the despotic governor, Lord Cornbury, and held in jail for six weeks. He successfully defended himself on the grounds that his license to preach, granted in Barbados and validated in Virginia, was valid in any colony. Though the court freed him, Cornbury made him pay all the costs of the trial.[3]

Migration from Ulster provided the largest number of Presbyterians. James I had seized nearly 3,800,000 acres of land in northern Ireland which he divided into two thousand-acre estates on condition that the owners bring in Scottish settlers. By 1641 there were about one hundred thousand of these settlers. In 1688 the Irish church had eighty ministers and nearly one hundred congregations in five presbyteries with a total membership of approximately two hundred thousand. From 1710 until just before the American Revolution, about two hundred thousand of these Scotch-Irish migrated to America because of the onerous economic and other restrictions placed upon them by the English government after 1689. They settled in New England, the middle colonies, such as Ulster and Orange counties in New York, but most made their way into Pennsylvania and down the valley of the Appalachians.

German Religious Pluralism in the Middle Colonies

When the Revolution began in 1776, it has been estimated that the Germans made up one-tenth of the population with one-third of them settled in Pennsylvania. Because of freedom of religion granted by Penn, Pennsylvania became a refuge for smaller German religious bodies of oppressed people.

German Mennonites were among the first to come to Germantown. A German lawyer, Francis Pastorius, became the agent of a land company which obtained twenty-five thousand acres after Penn visited Germany. In 1683 the first shipload of Mennonites from the Rhine area came to Germantown, now a suburb of Philadelphia. Many Swiss Mennonites settled in Lancaster County. All these people were from branches of the Anabaptist churches of the Reformation, which repudiated the state church principle, creeds and infant baptism in favor of a pure church of adult believers. They were often pacifistic and were opposed

[3]*Ibid.*, I, 256-261.

to oaths in court and to government control over what they thought were private matters.

The Taufers or Dunker German Baptists, who believed in trine immersion, love feasts and foot washing, were led to this country from the lower Rhine through the efforts of the Frankfort Land Company and of Penn's agents. Groups were led by Peter Becker and Alexander Mack, until about twenty congregations, some numbering two hundred, had arrived. Christopher Saur, who published the first German newspaper in the colonies and an edition of the German Bible in 1734, was one of this group. So also was Johann C. Beissel, who left the Dunkers about 1732 to found the semimonastic communal Ephrata Society. He opposed marriage and emphasized the seventh day (Saturday) as the day of rest. Separate buildings were erected for men and for women. After his death in 1758 the community declined quickly.

The Schwenkfelders, the followers of Kaspar Schwenkfeld, also came to Pennsylvánia in 1734. He taught that to the Bible should be added the continuing revelation of the Living Word by the Holy Spirit. One might speak of them as inner light Anabaptists who rejected the sacraments. In 1782 they organized themselves into a church.

The Moravians constituted a still larger group. They were originally followers of John Huss and were known as *Unitas Fratrum* or Unity of the Brethren. Under the leadership of Christian David they migrated in 1722 to Berthelsdorf, the estate of Count Zinzendorf (1700-1760). The Count, who emphasized missions and ecumenical fellowship, tried to link them with the Lutheran church. The Moravian church emerged in 1727, and Zinzendorf himself became a bishop in 1737. Promise of a free passage and land in Georgia led, in 1735, to initial founding of a colony there; but disease, death, and their refusal to bear arms led to the Moravians accepting Whitefield's offer of passage to Philadelphia on his sloop. They settled at Nazareth and Bethlehem in 1740 on land which Whitefield was in the process of purchasing. Zinzendorf visited the thriving settlement in 1741 and sought to unify the German groups in Pennsylvania into an evangelical alliance, but suspicion of his motives prevented this. However, he stimulated the Moravians to missionary work among the Indians. David Zeisberger was the foremost of many missionaries to the Indians in the area.

The established churches of the European Reformation, especially the Calvinistic and the left-wing groups, provided many settlers for America. A number of the leaders, such as Christopher Saur and David Zeisberger, helped to promote American culture and to bring the gospel to the Indians.

BIBLIOGRAPHY

OLMSTEAD. *HRUS*. Pp. 118-154.
SWEET. *SRA*. Pp. 83-94, 102-126.

Lutheranism:

MUHLENBERG, HENRY. *The Journals of Henry Melchior Muhlenberg*. Translated by T. G. Tappert and John W. Doberstein. Philadelphia: Evangelical Lutheran Ministerium of Pennsylvania and Adjacent States and the Muhlenberg Press, 1942. Interesting source of information concerning early Lutheranism in the middle colonies.

WENTZ, ABDEL R. *A Basic History of Lutheranism in America*. Philadelphia: Muhlenberg Press, 1955.

Presbyterianism:

ARMSTRONG, MAURICE, LOETSCHER, LEFFERTS A., and ANDERSON, CHARLES A. (eds.). *The Presbyterian Enterprise: Sources of American Presbyterian History*. Philadelphia: The Westminster Press, 1956. Useful collection of important documents of Presbyterian history.

LOETSCHER, LEFFERTS A. *A Brief History of the Presbyterians* (rev.). Philadelphia: The Westminster Press, 1958. Brief popular account.

SLOSSER, GAIUS J. (ed.). *They Seek a Country*. New York: The Macmillan Co., 1955. A full account of Presbyterianism in the United States with helpful charts of schisms and reunions.

TRINTERUD, LEONARD J. *The Forming of an American Tradition*. Philadelphia: The Westminster Press, 1949. The story of American Presbyterianism from 1706 to 1758.

Mennonites:

SMITH, C. HENRY. *The Story of the Mennonites* (3rd ed., rev. by Cornelius Krahn). Newton, Kan.: Mennonite Publication Office, 1950.

6

THE GREAT AWAKENING

THE GREAT AWAKENING was not only the first significant intercolonial movement in America, but it was also a part of an international Teutonic nonsectarian revival. This revival manifested itself in Germany under the ministry of Philip Spener (1635-1705), whose Pietism was an attempt to add devotion and zeal to coldly orthodox Lutheranism. Pietism influenced the Wesleys, who with Whitefield were leaders in the Methodist Awakening in early eighteenth century England.

The Great Awakening started with the work of the Dutch pastor Frelinghuysen and the Tennents among the Reformed in the middle colonies, spread to New England Congregationalism under Edwards, and then manifested itself in the southern colonies to the special benefit of the Methodists. It seems to have been a spontaneous spiritual movement with none of the planning so characteristic of mass urban evangelism since the Civil War. For a time it even helped to arrest the decline of New England Puritanism. It was only the first of a series of revival movements which seemed to emerge in a period of social crisis and spiritual need. It met the needs of a mobile frontier society which needed a personal, voluntary decision of commitment to religion because of the absence of strong religious institutional organization.

There were several reasons why revival seemed essential. The waning of religion and the rise of drunkenness and loose living find ample testimony in the sermons of the late seventeenth and early eighteenth centuries. The colonists had taken special part in the series of intercolonial wars between 1689 and 1763 with consequent deterioration of morals and religion. Efforts at political centralization by the British government caused much political unrest. The Half-Way Covenant and the practice of Stoddard in Northampton were evidences of spiritual decline. Migration to the frontier and the mobility of the population there left many without the beneficent influence of religion. People who were not born into a state church had to be brought into the Christian church by the voluntary, personal, spiritual rebirth which the Greak Awakening provided.

Revival in the Middle Colonies

Theodorus J. Frelinghuysen (1691-1747) ignited the fire of revival in his Dutch Reformed congregations in the Raritan River valley of New Jersey shortly after his arrival in the colony in 1720. Though he was opposed by other ministers, who wrote their *Complaint* against him, the revival continued and spread to Presbyterian congregations in the area by 1726. Frelinghuysen used prayer meetings for the converted and enlisted lay helpers.

William Tennent, the Scottish Presbyterian minister mentioned previously, had by 1728 established his "log college" at Neshaminy near Philadelphia and was training his sons Gilbert, John and William, Jr., along with Samuel Blair and others for the ministry. Gilbert (1703-1764) went to the New Brunswick Presbyterian church in New Jersey and became interested in the work of Frelinghuysen. Gilbert's flaming doctrinal preaching and his careful pastoral guidance soon provided leadership for revival. So many were converted that in 1738 the New Brunswick Presbytery was constituted, with five of the "log college" men as the founders. Revival spread throughout New Jersey and into New York and Pennsylvania, although not without opposition which led to a schism in the Presbyterian church in 1741. Gilbert Tennent's sermon in 1740, "The Danger of an Unconverted Ministry,"[1] and the emotional excesses of James Davenport, a pastor in Long Island, were factors in creating this opposition.

Revival in New England

Revival in New England must be linked with the name of Jonathan Edwards (1703-1758), who was possibly the greatest theologian America has had. He went to Yale at the age of thirteen, read Locke's essay "Concerning Human Understanding" at fourteen, earned his A.B. at seventeen, and then served as pastor of a Scottish Presbyterian church in New York. Later he was a tutor for three years at Yale. In 1727 he married the beautiful and talented Sarah Pierpont and that year became co-pastor of the Northampton church with his grandfather Solomon Stoddard. When Stoddard died in 1729, Edwards became the pastor and so remained until 1750.

[1] H. Shelton Smith *et al., American Christianity* (New York: Charles Scribner's Sons, 1960), I, 321-328.

Late in 1734 Edwards began a series of sermons on justification by faith, which were the fruit of his regular thirteen hours of study a day. He emphasized man's unworthiness and complete dependence upon God. The revival began with the conversion of a careless young woman whose experience seemed to awaken many between 1734 and 1735. Edwards' book *A Faithful Narrative*,[2] was published by 1738 as a description of the phenomena of the revival and to answer opponents. From this frontier church the revival moved eastward in New England. On July 8, 1741, Edwards preached his famous sermon, "Sinners in the Hands of an Angry God" (Deut. 32:35). Because Edwards openly cited in the pulpit the names of children of leading members of his church who had gotten hold of a book on midwifery in 1744, and because he would not admit any but the converted to the communion, he was forced to leave his church in 1750.

He moved to Stockbridge from Northampton as an Indian missionary and preached to the Indians and the settlers. His *Freedom of the Will* (1754) was written during this period. In this defense of Calvinism against Arminianism, Edwards emphasized the sovereignty of God. He wrote that man's will was naturally and rationally free, but lacked the moral ability to choose the right because of total depravity which left the will morally helpless. When the Holy Spirit would incline the will, then man was free to choose morally. Man had therefore a limited freedom of his will. Thus Edwards tried to link divine sovereignty and human responsibility but, in so doing, somewhat modified the Calvinistic system. Edwards also planned and partly wrote the *History of the Work of Human Redemption*, which he thought would be his greatest contribution to theology.

In 1758 Edwards moved to Princeton to become its president upon the death of the former president, his son-in-law, Aaron Burr, Sr., but he died that same year of a smallpox vaccination. Edwards was both philosopher and leader of the New England revival.

The coordinator of the Great Awakening in the colonies was George Whitefield (1714-1770), who was converted in college in 1735, spent a brief period in Georgia as a missionary, and returned to England, where his preaching aroused widespread interest. He pioneered open-air preaching and introduced Wesley to this technique. He returned to America in 1739 at the height of the

[2]Peter G. Mode, *Sourcebook and Bibliographical Guide to American Church History* (Menasha, Wis.: George Banta Publishing Co., 1921), pp. 214-217.

New England revival and was soon preaching to large crowds,
such as the nearly six thousand who on one occasion listened
to him on Boston Commons. His twin passions were evangelism
and social action. The latter found expression in his work to
collect money for, build and manage his orphanage at Savannah.
He worked with men of all denominations but specially admired
Gilbert Tennent and Jonathan Edwards. It was observation
of Edwards' happy homelife that made him determine to seek a
wife. Whitefield's strong voice and dramatic gifts were used
to carry the torch of revivalism up and down the American coast.
Between 1740 and 1742, over twenty-five thousand in a population
of three hundred thousand were added to the church in New
England.

Revival in the Southern Colonies

The Awakening spread to *Presbyterians* in Virginia after 1740.
Samuel Morris of Hanover began to read religious books, such
as Luther's *Commentary on Galatians,* to his neighbors, and some
were converted. So many came to this reading that he built a
reading house. Popular demand brought other houses into
being. In 1743 William Robinson, a Presbyterian minister, visited
Hanover, and these people were organized into Presbyterian
churches. Samuel Davies (1723-1761) was made the pastor in
1748, and under him the revival spread until he was called to
the presidency of Princeton in 1758. This revival thus gave Presbyterianism a hold in the South, but the Baptists and Methodists
became even stronger because of the revival.

There were few *Baptists* in Virginia in 1759, but by the time
of the American Revolution there were about ten thousand and
in 1790 nearly twenty thousand. In 1755, soon after Shubal
Stearns (1706-1771) moved with a few Separate Baptists to Sandy
Creek in North Carolina,[3] it became the scene of an emotional
revival, characterized by such phenomena as jerking, falling,
rolling, barking, and crying. The spread of the Baptist phase of
the revival was promoted by Daniel Marshall, Stearns's brother-in-
law, in spite of persecution from the established Anglican church.
In 1758 several Separate Baptist churches were organized into
the Sandy Creek Association. The revival also spread into Virginia. The more democratic polity and popular farmer-preacher
ministry gave the Baptists an advantage on the Kentucky frontier.

[3]Smith, op. cit., I, 362-366.

Union of the Separate with the Regular Baptists in 1801 began what has become the Southern Baptist Convention.

Methodism in the colonies began in New York in 1766 with services held in his home by Philip Embury (1728-1773), a carpenter and a Methodist lay preacher. This was at the request of his cousin, Barbara Heck. They were helped by Captain Webb of the British army, who was responsible for the beginning of Methodism in Philadelphia. Robert Strawbridge, an Irish immigrant, began to preach at Sam's Creek in Maryland and, about 1760, organized a Methodist society. Wesley also sent over Richard Boardman and Joseph Pilmoor to the middle colonies, but Pilmoor went on an extensive tour of the South.

John King and Robert Williams, Methodist local preachers, came to America in 1768. When Williams went to Virginia, he discovered that a revival was already in progress under the leadership of Devereux Jarratt (1733-1801), an Anglican clergyman of Bath Parish in Dinwiddie County. Jarratt's emotional and evangelical ministry won many converts whom he organized into societies. He warmly welcomed the Methodist lay preacher Robert Williams and set up societies and class meetings in 1774, because Methodism was still considered a part of the Anglican church. By 1777 more than three-fifths of all the colonial Methodists were in Virginia. Francis Asbury (1745-1816), who organized the circuit-rider system of American Methodism, came to America in 1771. He rode about two hundred seventy thousand miles and spoke about sixteen thousand times during his life. Thus it was the Great Awakening which made Methodism such a strong force in the colonies that it could emerge in 1784 as the earliest church with a national organization. This action was a disappointment to Jarratt.

Results of Revival

Consideration of the major results of the revival is important. It naturally created division of opinion which led in many cases to schism and division. The division of the Presbyterians in the middle colonies into the New Side prorevival church and the Old Side antirevival group occurred in 1741. The issues were whether earnest but untrained men who had neither college nor seminary degrees, but who were greatly used in the Awakening, could be licensed to preach by the presbytery, which alone could ordain, and whether men could itinerate from parish to parish without the consent of the minister in the parish. In 1741 the

Old Side synod of Philadelphia excluded several New Side Scotch-Irish ministers, who joined with other presbyteries to form the Synod of New York in 1745. When the groups finally reunited in 1758, the New Side had more than tripled the number of ministers while the Old Side had a few less ministers than in 1745.

Schism also occurred in New England Congregationalism. The Old Light group, led by Charles Chauncy, pastor of the First Church of Boston, opposed itinerant preachers of revivalism, lay exhorters and doctrinal looseness. The New Light group, including such men as Jonathan Edwards, was in favor of revival and supported revealed theology. It stood for the New England theology or the new divinity. Later exponents, Samuel Hopkins and Timothy Dwight, came to favor a general rather than the limited atonement, such as Edwards had been inclined to hold. The Old Light group became more liberal, with John Taylor denying total depravity but not actual sin. In time the Unitarian church was to emerge from this wing of Congregationalism in New England.

The Great Awakening also stimulated the rise of sectarian educational institutions which were to serve America well before the advent of state-supported institutions. Partly because of the expulsion of David Brainerd from Yale in his senior year and partly to provide an institution to train ministers for the New Side Presbyterians, a charter was obtained in 1746 for the College of New Jersey (Princeton). The college opened in 1747 in Jonathan Dickinson's home in Elizabethtown, New Jersey. It was moved to Newark that same year to meet in the home of its president, Aaron Burr. Gilbert Tennent and Samuel Davies raised four thousand pounds in England for it in 1754. The college was later moved to its present location in Princeton. The tabernacle erected in Philadelphia for Whitefield's services became the home of an academy in 1751. This was the nucleus of the University of Pennsylvania, which came into being in 1791. King's College (Columbia) began in 1754. The Dutch Reformed church opened Queen's College (Rutgers) in 1766. The Baptists established the College of Rhode Island (Brown) in 1764. Dartmouth was incorporated in 1769 to train men for work among the Indians. The Presbyterians' Washington and Lee College and Hampden-Sydney College had their beginnings in Virginia in 1774 and 1776. The training of ministers was one of the main functions of all these colleges.

Missionary work among the Indians, which had been first tried by the Mayhew family and John Eliot, was stimulated by the Awakening. Jonathan Edwards from 1750 to 1758 succeeded John Sargent, who had been a missionary at Northampton among the Housatonic Indians. Dartmouth College grew out of Moor's Indian Charity School which had been opened to train Indians to minister to their own people.

David Brainerd (1718-1747), who had but a brief ministry ended by tuberculosis, was ordained by the Presbytery of New York in 1744 after he had been expelled by Yale in 1742 for criticism of the spiritual state of one of his tutors. His best work was done among Indians near Trenton, New Jersey. In 1747 he went to the home of Jonathan Edwards whose daughter Jerusha was his fiancée. After Brainerd died, Edwards published his diary. William Carey, Henry Martyn, Samuel Marsden and Thomas Coke were all inspired to engage in missionary work after reading it.

Humanitarian work was another outcome of the revival. Whitefield created the Bethesda Orphanage at Savannah in 1741. In all his evangelistic meetings he collected money for this social expression of Christianity.

One should not forget that the Great Awakening stimulated intercolonial cooperation in the area of religion. This set a pattern that could be followed later in political and military cooperation among the colonies.

The Great Awakening was the first and very important manifestation of periodic waves of revival which have characterized American Christianity. It was to be followed by the Second Awakening at the end of the eighteenth century, after the crisis of revolution against the mother country and the surge of Deism which so harmed the religious life of the new nation.

BIBLIOGRAPHY

OLMSTEAD. *HRUS.* Pp. 155-190.
SWEET. *SRA.* Pp. 127-154, 159-171.

General Works on American Revivals:

BEARDSLEY, FRANK G. *A History of American Revivals.* Boston: American Tract Society, 1904.

MCLOUGHLIN, WILLIAM G. *Modern Revivalism: Charles Grandison Finney to Billy Graham.* New York: Ronald Press Co., 1959. Interesting, highly critical account of American revivalism—inaccurate in spots.

SWEET, WILLIAM W. *Revivalism in America, Its Origin, Growth and Decline*. New York: Charles Scribner's Sons, 1944. A scholarly general account.

WEISBERGER, BERNARD A. *They Gathered at the River*. Boston: Little, Brown and Co., 1958. A critical but interesting account of revivals with a helpful bibliography.

The Great Awakening:

BELDEN, ALBERT D. *George Whitefield—The Awakener*. New York: The Macmillan Co., 1953. Presents Whitefield as an evangelist and philanthropist.

FRELINGHUYSEN, PETER H. B. *Theodorus Jacobus Frelinghuysen*. Princeton: Princeton University Press, 1938.

GAUSTAD, EDWIN S. *The Great Awakening in New England*. New York: Harper & Brothers, 1957.

GEWEHR, WESLEY M. *The Great Awakening in Virginia, 1740-1790*. Durham, N.C., Duke University Press, 1930.

HENRY, STUART C. *George Whitefield: Wayfaring Witness*. New York: Abingdon Press, 1957.

MAXSON, CHARLES H. *The Great Awakening in the Middle Colonies*. Gloucester, Mass.: Peter Smith, reprint, 1958.

MILLER, PERRY. *Jonathan Edwards*. New York: William Sloane Associates, Inc., 1949. Emphasis on the intellectual influence of Locke on Edwards.

WINSLOW, OLA E. *Jonathan Edwards, 1703-1758, A Biography*. New York: The Macmillan Co., 1941. Able account of Edwards' role in the Great Awakening.

Baptists:

LUMPKIN, WILLIAM L. *Baptist Foundations in the South*. Nashville: Broadman Press, 1961.

Methodists:

ASBURY, FRANCIS. *Journals and Letters*. Edited by Elmer E. Clark, J. Manning Potts and John S. Payton. Nashville: Abingdon Press, 1958.

ASBURY, HERBERT. *A Methodist Saint: The Life of Bishop Asbury*. New York: Alfred A. Knopf, 1927.

CAMERON, RICHARD M. *The Rise of Methodism: A Source Book*. New York: Philosophical Library, 1954. Contains many useful documents.

CLARK, ELMER T. *An Album of Methodist History*. New York: Abingdon-Cokesbury Press, 1952. Excellent pictures and history of American Methodism in America in Part II.

LUCCOCK, HALFORD E., HUTCHINSON, PAUL, and GOODLOE, ROBERT W. *The Story of Methodism*. New York: Abingdon-Cokesbury Press, 1949. A popular history.

SWEET, WILLIAM W. *Methodism in American History* (2nd ed. rev.). New York: Abingdon Press, 1954.

———. (ed.). *The Methodists, 1783-1840, A Collection of Source Materials*. Chicago: University of Chicago Press, 1946.

THE RISE AND DECLINE OF ECCLESIASTICAL NATIONALISM
(1776-1876)

7

THE CHURCHES IN THE AMERICAN REVOLUTION

ALTHOUGH POLITICAL and economic problems were important factors in the coming of the American Revolution, there is considerable evidence that religious considerations also had an important part in the causes and course of the Revolution. Because the minister usually had the best education, the pulpit helped to mold public opinion before and during the Revolution. John Locke's political philosophy and biblical concepts of the state were linked to justify revolution.

Religion and the Causes of the Revolution

The Great Awakening negatively aided the Revolution by drawing off many former Anglicans into other churches opposed to the status quo. Many of Jarratt's converts became Methodists with little attachment to the Anglican church. In a positive manner the revival helped to break down provincialism and foster a sense of intercolonial unity. Common emotional and intellectual interests were fostered by the widespread travels of Whitefield, Gilbert Tennent and others who went up and down the Atlantic seaboard. Whitefield emphasized intercolonial religious cooperation.

Fear of Roman Catholic control of areas important to the thirteen colonies developed because the Quebec Act of 1774 put the area between the Mississippi and the Ohio Rivers within the boundaries of Quebec. This would bring Roman Catholicism very close to the middle and New England colonies.

The danger of English political control in the colonies by the establishment of a colonial Anglican episcopate in America received much attention from the pulpits of the day. Because such an appointment would be made by the British government, many of the colonists looked upon this as another ground for interference by the British government in the affairs of the colonies. The fact that there was little opposition to an Anglican bishop after the Revolution would seem to substantiate this view. One of the bitterest attacks upon the Anglican church was made by a Boston pastor, Jonathan Mayhew, who opposed both an Anglican bishop and the missionaries of the Society for the Propagation of the Gospel as possible agents to destroy Presbyterian and other free churches. This feeling against an Anglican bishop and missionaries as agents of British control was strongest in the New England and middle colonies.

The political philosophy which was behind the Revolution was strongly proclaimed from many pulpits. The political ideals of the English Revolution of 1688, which led the English to set up a limited monarchy and which were so eloquently portrayed by John Locke in his *Two Treatises of Government* (1690), were set forth in thanksgiving and election sermons and weekly lectures in the churches. The Bible, classical writers, such as Aristotle, Plato and Cicero, and the political ideas of the reformers were, along with Locke's works, sources for these sermons.

Government by the sovereign people was based upon fundamental natural rights which were a part of the law of nature apprehensible by reason and were also to be found in the divine revelation in the Bible. For the better organization of society, people who had these rights associated themselves by means of a church covenant and a civil compact in church and state. The Mayflower Compact followed the lines of a church covenant. Because God was the only absolute sovereign who had given delegated sovereignty to the people, who in turn by the compact or contract had granted it to their government, the people had the right to resist forcibly any illegal acts of government which violated the natural or written law of God. From the passage of the Stamp Act to the Declaration of Independence many ministers, particularly in the Congregational and Presbyterian churches, enunciated these principles which would justify the right of resistance against English royal tyranny.

The Churches in the Revolution

People and pastors in several of the denominations supported the cause of the Revolution with fervor and at the expense of personal sacrifice—in some cases at the cost of life. Few were more fervent than the Congregationalists of New England. Most of the clergy were graduates of Harvard or Yale. Election sermons before the governor and assembly were given as early as 1633 in Massachusetts, and the practice soon spread to other colonies. The burden of many of these sermons was that the people, who are the only source of political authority, have the right to resist usurpation of tyrants.

When the war broke out, these pastors proved that their sermons on civil matters were more than empty theory by recruiting volunteers and by serving as chaplains during the war. Timothy Dwight urged enlistment upon the students of Yale. John Cleaveland, of Ipswich, Massachusetts, was credited with persuading all the able-bodied men of his parish to enlist and then marching off to war with them.

The Presbyterians, particularly the Scotch-Irish, who were nearly a third of the three million in the colonies in 1776, and who remembered English trade limitations and religious discrimination against them before they migrated from Ulster, were ardent supporters of the revolutionary cause. There was considerable truth in Horace Walpole's statement that Cousin America had run off with a Presbyterian pastor. George Duffield's sermons in the Third Presbyterian Church of Philadelphia in 1775 impressed John Adams as being similar to those he had heard from the New England Congregational clergy.

John Witherspoon (1723-1794), who was born and educated in Edinburgh, was a minister of the Church of Scotland for nearly twenty-six years. He was called to the presidency of the College of New Jersey, which he served in that capacity from 1768 to 1794. His travels on behalf of the college took him to all parts of the colonies. James Madison, who became the fourth president of the United States, a vice-president, ten cabinet members, twelve governors, sixty congressmen, and three Supreme Court judges had been among Witherspoon's former students. He was a member of the second Continental Congress and the only ministerial signer of the Declaration of Independence and of the Articles of Confederation. He was also a member of several important committees of the Congress. His relations with Washington were always cordial. He served as a member of the New Jersey constitutional convention, which ratified the Constitution in 1787. The choice of Witherspoon as presiding officer of the first General Assembly of the Presbyterian church was also a testimony to his stature in American history. He was an equally earnest and sincere Christian in affairs of state and church.

Other Presbyterian pastors served the cause of revolution by proclamation of its principles long before the declaration of American independence, by recruiting soldiers and by service as chaplains. James Caldwell (1734-1781), pastor at Elizabethtown, became chaplain of a New Jersey regiment. When his men ran low on wads for their muskets, he secured Watts's hymnals from a nearby church to make wads for the guns. Perhaps Joseph Galloway was partly right in his belief that England's enemies were Congregationalists, Presbyterians and smugglers.

Because the Lutherans had no clear-cut organization in America, their service to the Revolution has to be linked with the work of individuals. Although Henry Muhlenberg remained neutral, his son John Peter, a pastor in Virginia, after preaching a sermon, pulled off his pulpit robes to reveal the uniform of a Virginian colonel. Most of the Lutherans were loyal to the revolutionary cause.

Because the Baptists had suffered persecution at the hands of Anglicans and had upheld freedom of conscience, separation of church and state, and the sovereignty of the people, they were ardent supporters of the Revolution. Both in Virginia and New England, Baptists used the Revolution to advance the cause of religious liberty. No Baptist was ever on the list of the enemies of the patriotic cause.

The Dutch Reformed church suffered greatly for its loyalty by destruction of church property and the scattering of its people, since its churches were mainly located in the early theater of war in New York. Two of its churches were used for a hospital and a riding school. Most of the German Reformed were loyal to the Whig cause. Michael Schlatter was even imprisoned for his loyal stand.

Largely because of the influence of the Carroll family of Maryland, the Roman Catholics, especially in Maryland and Pennsylvania, fought for the Revolutionary cause. Charles Carroll was one of the signers of the Declaration of Independence. Roman Catholic conduct in the Revolution taught the Protestant colonists that such people could be good citizens, neighbors and friends at the same time that they were loyal Roman Catholics.

The Anglican church was divided both by class and area in its loyalty to the war. Although many of the clergy in Virginia were Loyalists, the laymen overwhelmingly supported the Revolution. Loyalties were divided between Whig and Tory in the middle colonies, while in New England both clergy and laity were mainly Tory. Samuel Seabury, Jr., who became the first American bishop, fled from New York to the British side and became a chaplain in the British Army. On the other hand, William White of Philadelphia became chaplain of Congress. But most of the Anglican laymen were Whigs. About two-thirds of those who signed the Declaration of Independence were Anglicans.

Because of Wesley's Tory writings and his desire that the American Methodists should be neutral, the Methodists in America were looked upon with suspicion as Tories and persecuted. Most of Wesley's English preachers except Asbury returned to England. Even Asbury had to go into retirement in Delaware for part of the war. Some, such as Jason Lee, were pacifists, but others, especially in Virginia, stood by the revolutionary cause.

Some of the churches took no part in the Revolution because of their pacifism. The Friends or Quakers opposed both revolution and war, although some participated in what they called a defensive war. In the middle colonies they often suffered at the hands of the patriots but were treated more leniently in New England. Although favoring the Tory side, the Mennonites held to their pacifistic ideals even to the point of refusing to pay taxes to aid the war. The Moravians aided only in nonmilitary activities, such as providing their buildings for hospitals, the giving of supplies and keeping the Indians loyal to the colonial cause. Because of these activities, they were often mistreated by both sides.

The Continental Congress, beginning in 1775, declared by law fast days for prayer, and all sessions were opened with prayer. Divine worship was recommended in the Articles of War, and an American edition of the Bible, proposed by Robert Aitken, a printer of Philadelphia, was approved by Congress in 1783. Ministers recruited soldiers and either served as soldiers themselves or became chaplains. They were often important members of the committees of correspondence and served in constitutional conventions for the drafting of state constitutions.

This service to the colonial cause often cost them dearly, particularly in the war zones. Church buildings were destroyed and congregations scattered. Many able Tory ministers left the country, and wartime service took young men away from college and seminary. For the most part, the American churches carried more than their fair share of the burden of the Revolution.

BIBLIOGRAPHY

BALDWIN, ALICE M. *The New England Clergy and the American Revolution.* Durham, N.C.: Duke University Press, 1928. An ably documented account of the role of the Congregational clergy before and during the Revolution.

BREED, W. P. *Presbyterians and the Revolution.* Philadelphia: Presbyterian Board of Publication, 1876.

BRIDENBAUGH, CARL. *Mitre and Sceptre.* New York: Oxford University Press, 1962. A supplement to and updating of the account by Cross of the conflict between the colonists and England over ecclesiastical matters.

CROSS, ARTHUR L. *The Anglican Episcopate and the American Colonies.* Cambridge: Harvard University Press, 1924. The account of colonial fear of an Anglican bishop in America in relation to the Revolution.

OLMSTEAD. *HRUS.* Pp. 192-209.

SWEET. *SRA.* Pp. 172-188.

8

THE IMPACT OF THE REVOLUTION ON RELIGION

THE AMERICAN REVOLUTION brought great change in the relations between church and state. Before the Revolution the Anglican church was established in five southern colonies, in New York City and three counties, and the Congregational church was the state church of three New England colonies. Thus the churches were closely allied to the colonial governments. By 1786 in Virginia the church was separated from the state, and the practice spread to other colonies, with Massachusetts being one of the last to accept such separation in 1833. National church organization came rapidly at the end of the war.

Several factors played a part in the development of the climate of opinion which made these changes possible. The German, Scotch-Irish and Quaker immigrants, as well as the Baptists, were in favor of freer religious policies. The Great Awakening had promoted voluntary action of the layman in the field of religion. Pioneering on the frontier stimulated this spirit of independence. Locke's philosophy with its emphasis on the sovereignty of the people provided a rationalization for independent action.

Disestablishment in the New States

The struggle to disestablish the Anglican church in Virginia made allies of such diverse forces as the Deist leaders, including Jefferson, and the Baptists. More than half the population of Virginia was composed of dissenters. As early as 1776, without separating the church and state, the House of Burgesses had provided for religious freedom in Article 16 of the statement of fundamental principles of government. This brought petitions for disestablishment from Baptists, Presbyterians and Lutherans. By 1779 the act for state support of the Anglican clergy was repealed. Thomas Jefferson first presented a bill for separation of church and state in 1779, with the strong backing of the Baptists. This bill was passed in December, 1785, and became law in January, 1786.[1] Other legislation was soon added to work out the details of the separation. Thus by 1786 Virginia was added to New Jersey, Pennsylvania, Rhode Island and Delaware as colonies which had no state church. Other states soon followed the example of Virginia. While Maryland gave all Christians freedom of religion in the constitution of 1776, it was not until 1826 that this privilege was extended to the Jews. North Carolina provided for separation in 1776, and South Carolina followed suit in 1790. Georgia made its decision in 1777. By 1784 the Anglican church lost all its privileges in New York.

The Congregationalist establishments in New England gave way to separation of church and state more slowly. Baptists under the leadership of Isaac Backus (1724-1806), the religious historian of New England, and President Manning of Rhode Island College agitated vigorously for the limitation of Congregational privilege in New England. To the great disappointment of Lyman Beecher, the constitutional convention of 1818 separated church and state in Connecticut. New Hampshire had taken the same step a year earlier, in 1817, but not until 1833 did Massachusetts in a constitutional amendment disestablish the Congregational church. This step wiped out the last vestige of establishment of churches in the states of the new nation.

Separation of church and state in the states influenced the adoption of the principles of separation of church and state in the federal system and the provision of complete religious freedom in the Constitution. State churches became denominational churches and parts of national organizations. The loss of church subsidies made voluntary support of religion mandatory and strengthened the position of the laity. It also made evangelism more important as a technique to bring people into the churches. The American churches became completely independent of England in every respect.

The Organization of National Churches

Little activity to form national denominational organizations by the churches occurred before 1776, but the American Revolution left the Methodist churches without much leadership from England and free to set up the national organization which Wesley had suggested. The organization of a national *Methodist* church in America preceded national organization of that body

[1] Henry S. Commager (ed.), *Documents of American History* (4th ed.; New York: Appleton-Century-Crofts, Inc., 1948), pp. 125, 126.

in England by several years. As early as 1779 Asbury was recognized by Methodists in the North as their leader, and later by those in the South. Because he discovered that presbyters had ordained ministers in the early church, Wesley decided he could perform the functions of a bishop. In 1784, Wesley ordained Richard Whatcoat and Thomas Vasey as ministers who could administer the sacraments, and consecrated Thomas Coke as superintendent of the Methodist churches in America. Wesley wanted Coke and Asbury to serve as co-superintendents. He also prepared a liturgy, a hymnbook and a creed of twenty-four articles condensed from the Thirty-nine Articles of the Anglican church.

When Coke met Asbury, it was decided that a conference of the ministers must be called to consider Wesley's plan. About sixty of the eighty-four Methodist preachers met at the Christmas conference in Baltimore on December 24, 1784. It named the new church the Methodist Episcopal church. Because Asbury would not become superintendent except by choice of the American clergy, the meeting elected him and Coke as superintendents, and Asbury was ordained as deacon, elder and superintendent on three successive days. He very soon began to use the name bishop for his office. A creed of twenty-five articles was adopted, and the churches were organized in circuits and conferences. Plans were laid for a college, to be called Cokesbury. This was opened in Maryland in 1787.

A small group of Methodists split to form the Republican Methodists. James O'Kelly in 1792 wanted to permit ministers who did not like their appointments from the bishop to appeal to the Conference. When this was refused, he and his followers broke with the national church in 1794 and maintained their separate existence until they merged with the Christian movement of Barton Stone.

The *Anglican* church in the new nation was the most divided of the denominations and most dependent upon England for its leadership. The presence of so many Tories among the clergy brought it under suspicion of the authorities. Thus the first steps toward national organization in the states were taken slowly.

William Smith (1727-1803) of Maryland, who had manifested Tory sentiments during the war, called a conference in 1780 which was attended by three clergymen and several laymen. Successive assemblies adopted the name Protestant Episcopal church and elected Smith as their bishop, but he was never consecrated to that office. Perhaps this was fortunate in view of his reputed tippling tendencies.

Ten clergymen in Connecticut in 1783 elected Samuel Seabury (1729-1796) as bishop. Seabury was a graduate of Yale and had studied medicine at the University of Edinburgh. He was sent out to serve as a missionary and became a pastor in Long Island. His loyalty to England led him to become a British military chaplain during the Revolution. When he went to England for consecration, the Archbishop of Canterbury refused this service on the grounds that the act for ordination called for an oath of allegiance to the ruler. Seabury was then consecrated bishop by nonjuring bishops of Scotland in 1784. He was the first American to be so consecrated.

William White (1748-1836), who had been chaplain of the Continental Congress, later of Congress, and was now a clergyman of Christ Church in Philadelphia, became the leader in promoting a national Episcopal church. In 1782 he wrote a pamphlet setting forth a plan for a national organization, separated from the state and with lay representation in the governmental structure of the church. After preliminary meetings, a national gathering was held in New York in 1784, followed by a meeting of the first "general convention" in Philadelphia in 1785 in which New England was not represented. This meeting chose White and two others as bishops. A constitution[2] was developed, a prayer book adopted, the work of revising the liturgy was begun, and the name Protestant Episcopal Church of America was adopted. White and Samuel Provoost were consecrated as bishops in England in 1787.

At the General Convention in 1789, Seabury and the New England clergy were present. A constitution, a set of canons to provide laws for the church, a revised prayer book and the unification of the church on a national level were major results. This was mainly through the tact and zeal of Bishop White.

American *Presbyterians* had been independent of Old World Presbyterianism since the creation of the first presbytery in 1706. As early as 1785, the synod gave consideration to a national organization for the church. John Witherspoon became the leader in this movement for national organization. The synodical meeting of 1788 adopted the Form of Government, the Book of Dis-

[2]Peter G. Mode, *Sourcebook and Bibliographical Guide to American Church History* (Menasha, Wis.: George Banta Publishing Co., 1921), pp. 256-259.

cipline, the Westminster Confession of faith, the two catechisms and the Directory of Worship as the constitution of the national church. The first General Assembly of the national church met at Philadelphia in 1789, with Witherspoon serving as its presiding officer until the election of a moderator.

The *Dutch Reformed* congregations formed a national organization in 1792 which was completely independent of the church in Holland. Between 1792 and 1795 the *German Reformed* church created a system of church government, creeds and liturgy and became a national body. Not until 1820 did the *Lutherans* meet in a national General Synod. The synod was given power to advise the constituent synods and to coordinate educational and missionary activity on a national scale. The Lutheran laity were given representation in the above bodies. The *Moravian* church retained its ties with the parent body until 1857, when a national independent body was created. The *Quakers*, with their democratic local control and congregational system, did not feel the need for national organization.

The *Baptists* had cooperated nationally in support of the movement to separate church and state but formed their associations mainly on a state level. In Virginia, after the Revolution the Baptists created a general committee to coordinate their work, but this was the only step toward anything like a body that could speak for the Baptists of any area.

Because of the democratic local government of the New England *Congregational* churches and the growing schism between the unitarian and trinitarian groups, they formed no national organization.

About two-thirds of the more than thirty thousand *Roman Catholics* after the Revolution were in Maryland. They had supported the Revolution and separation of church and state after the war to gain their religious freedom. John Carroll (1735-1815), who had become a priest and had taught in Roman Catholic institutions in Belgium, led the movement for an American Roman Catholic organization free from the Vicar Apostolic in London. He was appointed Prefect Apostolic by the Pope in 1784, and the Roman Catholic church in America became independent of English control. Carroll was consecrated bishop of Baltimore in 1790 and archbishop in 1808.

After the Revolution lay representation was granted in many groups in which that had not been the case earlier.

Religion and the National Government

Religion also had its part in the formation of the Constitution. Most of the denominations were represented through the religious affiliations of the delegates to the national convention in Philadelphia in 1787. Article VI, Section 3 of the Constitution, which was proposed by Charles Pinckney, banned any religious test for office. This was apparently aimed at the Test Act of England, which provided that only those taking the Anglican communion could hold public office. The Northwest Ordinance of 1787 provided for freedom of conscience in the territories.[3]

The First Amendment to the Constitution provided that Congress could not prefer, give privileges to or establish any faith as a state faith. This amendment, submitted by James Madison in 1789, went into effect in 1791 and created the "wall of separation" between church and state which has been so tenaciously held by most Protestants since that time. The traditional American separation of church and state and freedom of religion and conscience for which Roger Williams and William Penn had stood depends on these various statements.

BIBLIOGRAPHY

OLMSTEAD. *HRUS. Pp.* 210-218, 221-236.
PFEFFER, LEO. *Church, State and Freedom.* Boston: Beacon Press, 1953.
STOKES, ANSON P. *Church and State in the United States.* 3 vols. New York: Harper & Brothers, 1950.
SWEET. *SRA.* Pp. 189-204.

[3]Commager, *op. cit.*, p. 130.

9

THE CHURCH ON THE FRONTIER

THE AREA EAST of the Alleghenies was the stage for American colonial religious history, but after the Revolution people poured into the West to take up the new lands. The church faced the challenge of meeting the spiritual needs of these migrants on a mobile frontier. On the individualistic frontier, certain churches, such as the Methodist and the Baptist, fared better than the other denominations in wooing the frontiersmen into the church.

The Task of the Church

Nearly 95 percent of the approximately 4,000,000 people in America were to be found in the thirteen new states in 1790. By 1820, 25 percent of a population of nearly 9,640,000 were outside the boundaries of the original thirteen colonies and, by 1850, 50 per cent of a population above 23,000,000 were outside this area. In 1790 only about 200,000 were west of the mountains, but by 1800, 380,000 were in that area. Between 1790 and 1830 it is estimated that New England alone lost about 800,000 people to the new western areas. By 1829 ten of the eleven new states admitted since 1791 were west of the Alleghenies. The family of Hamlin Garland moved successively from Maine to Wisconsin, Minnesota, Iowa and South Dakota. The family of the frontier historian Frederick Jackson Turner after several generations in Massachusetts moved from there to Connecticut, Vermont, New York, Michigan, Wisconsin and Nebraska.

Several factors contributed to this extensive migration. Peace terms in 1783 extended the area of the United States to the Mississippi River; and the increase of population from approximately three to four million between 1781 and 1790, in conjunction with economic distress along the seaboard, led many to try their fortune in the new area. More of this migration was from the southern highlands than from the North. The Northwest Ordinance of 1787, which brought into being a new technique for imperial development, stimulated the movement of population into the area north and west of the Ohio River. Whereas earlier, people in colonial areas remained as subjects, this act made it possible, when enough people were living in an area, to move through a territorial stage to statehood. The sale of Louisiana to the United States in 1803 added much land beyond the Mississippi to the area open for expansion. Jefferson's embargo on trade with the participants in the Napoleonic wars and the War of 1812 with England also created hard times, which further stimulated the flow of population westward. Many native Americans took advantage of these opportunities.

The problems of national organization, the need of revival and the necessity of meeting the spiritual needs of the frontiersmen were the major challenges to the church after the Revolution, but of these problems the last was probably the greatest. Most of the denominations made great efforts to rise to the challenge.

The changes in rank and membership reveal that some churches adapted better than others to the demands of the frontier. Beginning with about 700 congregations of Congregationalists, about 600 Presbyterian and lesser numbers of Baptist, Episcopalian, Quaker, Reformed, Lutheran, Roman Catholic and Methodist congregations in that order in 1790, the figures and ranking were drastically changed by 1850. The Methodists then ranked first with 1,324,000, the Baptists second with 815,000, the Presbyterians third with 487,000, the Congregationalists fourth, the Lutherans fifth, the Disciples sixth with 118,000 and the Episcopalians seventh. The two denominations that had been established churches in the colonial era fared poorly; but the Methodists, Baptists and Presbyterians were most successful on the frontier. The Baptist farmer-preacher went west with the people, the Methodist circuit rider was sent to them, and the Presbyterians called their pastors to new areas.

The Churches on the Frontier

The Presbyterians, with large numbers of Scotch-Irish on the frontier, were strategically situated to meet the needs of the new settlers. As early as 1781 Redstone Presbytery was formed as the first such organization west of the mountains. By 1802 three presbyteries were united into the Synod of Pittsburgh. David Rice was responsible for the growth of Presyterianism in

Kentucky until the Presbytery of Transylvania was organized. Three presbyteries were joined in the Synod of Kentucky in 1802.

The adoption of the Plan of Union[1] by the Presbyterians and Congregationalists in 1801 to prevent duplication of effort was even more important than the pioneer preachers in the growth of these denominations on the frontier. The tendency to Presbyterian polity in the Saybrook Platform of 1708 in Connecticut made such cooperation possible. The plan, proposed in 1800 in the Connecticut General Asociation, was adopted by the New England churches and the Presbyterian church in 1801. Settlers of both churches could form a congregation with the polity and discipline of the majority group as their guide in organization, and could call a minister of either denomination who would still remain a minister of his own denomination. Provision was made for equitable settlement of disputes. Begun in New York, this plan worked to the advantage of the Presbyterians in most instances. But even this advantage did not prevent the Presbyterians from falling behind the Baptists and Methodists in rank and numbers. Their rigid doctrine and polity, the formality of their services and the immobility of the Presbyterian pastor may have been factors in this situation.

Congregationalism in New England remained wedded to establishment and privilege and therefore complacent and superior, while the other churches were busy on the frontier. The sectional outlook which confined its vision to New England prevented it from seeing the need of the eight hundred thousand who had moved from New England to the frontier between 1790 and 1820. The loose polity and the Plan of Union permitted the Presbyterians to absorb most of the Congregationalists on the frontier.

The Baptists fared even better numerically than the Presbyterians did. Persecution, depression, and the lure of cheap land drew west more Baptists, many of whom were of the poorest class. Often whole congregations migrated with their farmer-preacher, who farmed during the week and ministered on Sunday. Freedom from centralized control and democratic autonomy of the local congregation in Baptist polity appealed to the individualism of the frontier. More Baptist preachers were available, as anyone with ability might be licensed to preach without extensive training. Their doctrine was simple compared to some denominations, and their frontier preacher spoke the language of the

[1]Peter G. Mode, *Sourcebook and Bibliographical Guide to American Church History* (Menasha, Wis.: George Banta Publishing Co., 1921), pp. 421, 422.

common person so that he could make religion intelligible to anyone.

Severns Valley Church, formed in 1781, was the first Baptist church west of the mountains. Lewis Craig and his congregation moved from Virginia to Kentucky. By 1785 six Baptist churches were able to unite into the first western association, the Elkhorn Association. Growth was rapid from this time on.

Methodists were even more successful than the Baptists. Their system of organizing converts in the local society into classes of twelve under lay leadership, their use of lay preachers to man the societies, and the circuit rider system of making one man responsible for several societies gave them great advantage despite their highly centralized system. The circuit riders came to the cabins of the people. Peter Cartwright (1785-1872) was an excellent illustration of a Kentucky convert who was licensed as a lay preacher, ordained, rode circuit in Kentucky and Illinois and finally became a bishop. Circuits might involve a month or more of riding up to four hundred miles, and numerous sermons, while all the time the rider endured real hardships. Free will and free grace of Arminian Methodism made a greater appeal than predestination to the individualistic frontiersman. Besides, in Asbury they had a great leader and, after 1784, they had an efficient national organization. It is little wonder that by 1850 they were the largest denomination.

The exclusion of slavery from the Northwest by the ordinance of 1787 brought many Quakers, especially from the southern slave states, to that area. Ohio and Indiana attracted nearly fifty thousand Quakers by 1845. Their exclusiveness, however, hindered any large-scale growth.

The other established body of prerevolutionary America, the Episcopal church, was looked upon with suspicion because of its large number of Tories during the Revolution. It had lost many people and pastors. Philander Chase (1775-1852) founded Episcopalianism west of the mountains. After graduation from Dartmouth he became a missionary in New York, New Orleans, and Ohio. Here he organized the first diocese in 1817, of which he later became bishop, the first such bishop west of the mountains. He founded Kenyon College to give educational opportunity. But by 1850 the Episcopalian church still ranked only seventh among the churches.

The Roman Catholic church sent priests to its communicants in Kentucky and the future Indiana. In the former area Stephen

Badin was a leader, and Father Benedict Flaget in the latter. By 1808 a diocese was organized in Kentucky with Flaget as its bishop. But not until the great Irish and German migration of the 1840's was the Roman Catholic church to gain great numbers either east or west of the mountains.

The western migration had stimulated the church to the challenge of home missions. The Plan of Union was a tangible evidence of this interest in the spiritual welfare of the pioneer. The growth of democracy, lay participation in leadership, and a willingness to give generously to meet spiritual need were a part of the gains made by the churches. New churches, such as the Disciples and the Christians, especially illustrate these latter gains. Methodists and Baptists, however, were the most successful in the churches' response to the challenge of the masses on the frontier over the mountains.

BIBLIOGRAPHY

CARTWRIGHT, PETER. *Autobiography of Peter Cartwright.* New York: Abingdon Press, 1956.

OLMSTEAD. *HRUS.* Pp. 238-256.

PHARES, ROSS. *Bible in Pocket, Gun in Hand.* New York: Doubleday & Company, 1964.

SWEET. *SRA.* Pp. 205-222.

10

RELIGIONS OF THE HEAD
AND THE HEART

THE TWO decades after the Declaration of Independence were marked by a decline in spiritual fervor. This decline manifested itself in the deistic movement, which won the educated and later many of the masses to its banner. It was fortunate that it was followed by the revival of spiritual zeal of the Second Great Awakening. This began in southern and eastern colleges among the educated and spread by means of the camp meeting among the masses on the western frontier.

Deism in the United States

Deism was the belief in a transcendent God whose creation is run by natural laws discoverable by reason. Herbert of Cherbury (1583-1648) in his *De Veritate* (1624) first enunciated its basic doctrines as the worship of God, the necessity of virtue, and immortality with reward and punishment. Newton's concept of gravitation, a natural law unifying the field of physics, was analogically applied to religion and stimulated the search for a natural religion. In such a system there was no room for miracle and prayer, as they would involve invalidation of fixed natural laws. The deity of Christ was essentially denied.

Deism, which originated in England, spread quickly to the Continent where it was espoused by such men as Voltaire, Rousseau, and Condorcet of France, and Frederick the Great of Prussia. Liberal tendencies in New England Congregationalism, coupled with the importation of deistic literature from England and personal promulgation by the English and French officers during the course of the Revolution, won a following for Deism among the educated classes in America.

In 1800 Yale had only one church member among its graduates, and students delighted in calling each other by the names of great French Deists. Ethan Allen (ca. 1738-1789) opposed revealed religion in his book *Reason the Only Oracle of Man* (1784) and asserted that reason could produce a natural religion. Thomas Paine (1737-1809), the popular author of *Common Sense* (1776), which upheld the Revolution, wrote *The Age of Reason* (1794), in which he denied the validity of biblical revelation and the deity and Saviourhood of Christ. Elihu Palmer (1764-1806), a former Baptist minister who had been dismissed from the ministry on charges of heresy, became the popularizer of Deism for the masses. Men such as Thomas Jefferson and Benjamin Franklin added respectability to the vogue for Deism.

Although Deists were humanitarian and promoted reforms, such as Jefferson's achievement of separation of church and state in Virginia in 1786, and although they promoted education, as seen in the activities of such men as Franklin, who was mainly responsible for founding what became the University of Pennsylvania, Deism led to a drop in attendance at church services, to drunkenness and swearing in some cases, and to lack of ethical integrity. Especially when it spread to the frontier did it lead to an irreligious, careless life. Its influence was diminished and finally seriously checked by the Second Awakening.

The Second Awakening in the United States

Need of spiritual revitalization was evident by the end of the American Revolution and became more apparent during the next decade. Deistic influence played an important part in this decline, particularly in the educated portion of the population. The tough life of the frontier, with the problems of hostile Indians, homemade whiskey, disease and the lack of stabilizing influences such as schools and churches, provided no spiritual aid to frontiersmen. The brutalizing effects of war during the Revolution and the disruption of church life also played their part in the spiritual decline. This decline was reflected in the skepticism and infidelity within the leading colleges, such as Princeton, Yale and Harvard.

The Great Awakening had been characterized by a strong Calvinistic and more aristocratic tone with less display of emotion, but the Second Awakening was marked by Arminian and democratic tendencies. These promised salvation to all with more human responsibility and, particularly in the West, by more emotional display. Its peak period occurred from 1790 to approximately 1810.

Colleges along the seaboard became the centers in the South and East from which the revival radiated to the West. Students

in Hampden-Sydney College (Presbyterian) began to read religious books and hold prayer groups about 1787. Many students
were converted and the awakening spread to Washington College, now called Washington and Lee, another Presbyterian
school. More than half the student bodies of the two schools
were converted. Among these was Archibald Alexander, later
to become the great theologian of Princeton.

The most important awakening in the East took place at Yale
College. Timothy Dwight, who had been a chaplain during the
Revolutionary War and who became president of Yale in 1795,
challenged the skeptical student body with his lectures and
chapel sermons. Revival came in 1802 and of the two hundred
thirty students in Yale, about one-third were converted. The college was visited with periodic awakenings until 1820. Similar
revivals took place in Amherst, Dartmouth and Williams colleges.
Students carried the revival spirit to the churches of New England.

The lack of prominent leaders and excitement in the eastern
revival was unlike the leadership and emotional outbursts that
accompanied the outdoor revivals on the western frontier. James
McGready, a Scotch-Irish Presbyterian minister, seems to have
been mainly responsible for the awakening on the frontier. Between 1797 and 1800 revival came to his three congregations
in Logan County, Kentucky. People from all over the country
came to the sacramental service of 1800 in which the communion
was celebrated and new members admitted. Barton Stone, another Presbyterian minister, was present at the meeting, which
was characterized by much emotional and physical display.

Barton Stone carried news of this movement to his churches
at Cane Ridge, Kentucky, and in August, 1801, a camp meeting
was held at Cane Ridge. Estimates of those in attendance, some
from even as far away as Ohio, vary from ten thousand to twenty-
five thousand. This technique, which had been pioneered by the
Presbyterians, brought together people of all denominations from
distances of thirty to one hundred miles in their wagons, for a
period from Thursday to Tuesday, for preaching and for the cele-
bration of communion on Sunday. The interdenominational meeting at Cane Ridge was marked by great emotional display and
physical manifestations, such as falling, rapid jerking of the body
or head backward and forward or sideways, dancing, rolling on
the ground, running, and even barking like a dog. Many however,

seem to have been genuinely converted to a new life that left its mark for good on the frontier.[1]

This technique of the camp meeting became so useful and so congenial to the frontier need for social and religious gatherings, that by 1811 Asbury reported there were more than four hundred camp meetings, and by 1820 it was estimated that one thousand meetings of this nature were being held annually. Because of the emotional and physical extravagances, the Presbyterians ceased to use the camp meeting; but the Baptists and especially the Methodists made much use of it. The hymnody of the frontier camp meeting was often crude doggerel, and such large gatherings occasionally brought moral problems. But Kentucky travelers remarked on the improvement in morals in the area after the meetings were over. This was the heyday of the camp meeting. One notes that later revivals were generally held indoors, in churches and auditoriums.

In addition to the contribution of the camp meeting and the improvement in morals, the revival contributed to education. Andover Seminary was founded in 1807 to counteract the drift toward liberalism at Harvard. Princeton Seminary came into being in 1812. Many colleges were founded on the frontier, especially after the Dartmouth College case in 1819, in which the Supreme Court upheld the right of private colleges to be free from control by the state.

Schism was another outcome of the revival. The Cumberland Presbyterian church began in 1810. The Disciples of Christ under the leadership of Alexander Campbell and the Christians under Barton Stone were other groups which emerged in the disputes over revival and by schism from existing bodies.

As a result of the Awakening, large numbers were brought into the churches, particularly the Baptist and Methodist. The Presbyterians did not fare quite so well.

Both home and foreign missionary work was stimulated. The American Board of Commissioners for Foreign Missions came into being in 1810 as the result of the efforts of Adoniram Judson and his friends, such as Samuel Mills. Social reform was also stimulated. Lane Seminary, founded in 1823, soon became a center for antislavery agitation.

Publication of Christian literature was increased. The Ameri-

[1]Peter G. Mode, *Sourcebook and Bibliographical Guide to American Church History* (Menasha, Wis.: George Banta Publishing Co., 1921), pp. 336, 337.

can Bible Society and the American Tract Society worked on the provision of Bibles and Christian literature for those who were demanding such help because of the interest in religion developed by the revival.

Though there had been emotional and physical excesses in the revival, many lives were permanently transformed. Moral standards were elevated on the frontier. Thus the awakening left a positive impact for good which was beneficial to American life.

BIBLIOGRAPHY

OLMSTEAD. *HRUS*. Pp. 191, 218-221, 256-263.
SWEET. *SRA*. Pp. 223-231.

Deism:

MORAIS, HERBERT M. *Deism in Eighteenth Century America*. New York: Columbia University Press, 1934.

ORR, JOHN. *English Deism: Its Roots and Its Fruits*. Grand Rapids: Wm. B. Eerdmans Publishing Co., 1934. An excellent account of Deism.

The Second Awakening:

CLEVELAND, CATHARINE C. *The Great Revival in the West, 1797-1805*. Chicago: University of Chicago Press, 1916.

CUNNINGHAM, CHARLES E. *Timothy Dwight*. New York: The Macmillan Co., 1942.

JOHNSON, CHARLES A., *The Frontier Camp Meeting*. Dallas: Southern Methodist University Press, 1955. An excellent account of the camp meeting.

KELLER, CHARLES R. *The Second Great Awakening in Connecticut*. New Haven: Yale University Press, 1942.

11

NEW DENOMINATIONS

NEW DENOMINATIONS which appeared in the West were mainly a result of the Second Awakening. Others, emerging in the East, were based upon disagreement over the interpretation of the Bible and upon the individualistic spirit of the time. Schism in denominations resulted in new churches, but in some cases the division of opinion was contained within the denominations. The Presbyterians suffered the heaviest losses.

New Denominations in the West

Kentucky was the stage for the appearance of the Cumberland Presbyterian church in 1810. Many of the Presbyterian ministers, such as the McGees and McGready, had used the camp meeting with success and had modified Calvinistic doctrines along more democratic religious lines so that human responsibility was emphasized. To get the needed pastors to minister to the new converts in the West, it was necessary to lower educational standards for the ministry. Transylvania Presbytery in 1801 appointed four men "to exhort and catechize," and later licensed three more to preach in vacant pulpits. Some of the members of the presbytery objected to this irregular procedure because these men had not had the college and seminary training required of Presbyterian ministers. In addition, several of these men held doctrines which were Arminian in nature.

In 1805 the Synod of Kentucky sent a committee to look into the licensing of untrained men practiced by the Cumberland Presbytery. Because the presbytery refused to permit the committee to reexamine the candidates for licensure and also refused to permit some of its members to face charges before the synod, the synod dissolved the presbytery in 1806 and put its churches under the control of Transylvania Presbytery. Several recalcitrant members led by Finis Ewing and Samuel King met in February, 1810, and organized an independent Cumberland presbytery. By 1812 the church was big enough to form a synod. From 1810 until 1906 it maintained its independent existence, but in that year part of it reunited with the Presbyterian Church in the United States of America. The Cumberland Presbyterians used the camp meeting and circuit system and preached an evangelistic and modified Calvinism.

The present Disciples or Christian church owes its existence to the union in 1832 of the New Light or Christian schism of Barton Stone and the Campbellites or Disciples of Alexander Campbell. Kentucky and Ohio were the major strongholds of the New Lights.

Barton Stone (1772-1844), a North Carolinian Presbyterian, had preached in Kentucky and Tennessee until he took over the Cane Ridge church in 1796 and was ordained by the presbytery in 1798. Five ministers including Stone questioned the doctrines of election and limited atonement, and in 1803 Richard McNemar and John Thompson were tried by the Synod of Kentucky on charges of Arminianism. These two, Stone and two others protested that the Bible was the only rule of faith. Their pulpits were declared vacant and they were suspended. The five formed Springfield Presbytery in the fall of 1803 with the Bible as their standard. They dissolved their presbytery in 1804 with the semi-humorous document, "The Last Will and Testament of Springfield Presbytery,"[1] as an explanation for this action. They then formed the Christian church, to which Stone alone remained true. Two of the others defected to the Shakers and two returned to the Presbyterian church. Stone's Christian church grew rapidly in Ohio, Kentucky, Tennessee and Indiana. The Bible was to be the sole rule of faith and practice, the polity was to be congregational, immersion the proper form of baptism and the second coming of Christ was awaited with expectancy.

The Campbellites or Disciples were the followers of Thomas Campbell and his son Alexander of Pennsylvania. Thomas Campbell was a Scotch-Irish Antiburgher Presbyterian who migrated to America for reasons of health. He became a pastor in western Pennsylvania, but he refused to adhere to the requirement of a closed communion and invited all Presbyterians to participate. He left that church and with some friends in 1809 organized the Christian Association of Washington County, which held to the

[1]Peter G. Mode, *Sourcebook and Bibliographical Guide to American Church History* (Menasha, Wis.: George Banta Publishing Co., 1921), pp. 342-345.

sole authority of the Bible.[2] His son Alexander Campbell (1788-1866) arrived in that year and began to preach. In 1811 the Brush Run Church was organized with Alexander Campbell as the preacher after his ordination. The group adopted congregational church government, baptism by immersion, weekly communion and the doctrine of the imminent return of Christ, all of which they claimed were based upon the Scriptures. Between 1813 and 1830 they were loosely associated with the Baptists. Campbell and Stone, who first met in 1824, saw that their views were similar, and in 1832 the former Presbyterian leader led his New Light Christians to unite with the former Baptist Campbellites or Disciples under the name Christian or Disciples. They have grown rapidly since that union.

Germans with inclinations toward Methodist theology and polity founded two new groups in Pennsylvania. Philip W. Otterbein (1726-1813), a German Reformed minister, became a close friend of Asbury and adopted his techniques of class meetings and lay leaders. Martin Boehm, a former Mennonite, united with Otterbein to found the United Brethren in Christ church in 1800. This church with Methodist government and doctrine chose the two men as its first bishops.

Jacob Albright (1759-1808) preached to the Germans in Pennsylvania after his conversion and organized his converts into Methodist classes. His followers increased until in 1807, an annual conference known as the Evangelical Association, and later the Evangelical church, was formed. In 1946 these two Arminian and Episcopal bodies united as the Evangelical United Brethren Church, with a membership of more than seven hundred thousand.

Another church which became a frontier group emerged from a secession from the Dutch Reformed church. In 1834 congregations in Holland had left the state church because of its doctrinal laxness, and under the leadership of A. C. Van Raalte many of them later migrated to western Michigan. In 1857 some of these congregations in Michigan united to form what became the Christian Reformed church, a strongly Calvinistic body with its main center in Grand Rapids. Calvin College and Seminary are its major educational institutions.

Other groups, such as the Mormons and Adventists, also emerged on the frontier along with such communal sects as the Shakers. These will be given later consideration.

[2]*Ibid.*, pp. 345-347.

New Denominations in the East

Liberalizing tendencies in New England theology in the days of Jonathan Edwards have already been noticed. While Edwards' followers made more room for freedom of the will and human responsibility, Charles Chauncy (1705-1787) and his successors advocated theological ideas which resulted in the development of Unitarianism on the one side and the liberal ideas of Nathaniel Taylor (1786-1858) and Horace Bushnell (1802-1876)on the other. The ideas of the latter were to be influential later in the field of Christian education.

Nathaniel Taylor was a Congregational pastor in New Haven who became professor of theology at Yale in 1822. Moral depravity was to him an act of choice whereby man, a responsible moral agent, chooses sin apart from divine grace. Man is free to accept or reject salvation. Thus the atonement is not limited to the elect. His teachings were a factor in the origin of Hartford Seminary in 1834.

Both Universalism and Unitarianism represent the more radical side of liberal New England theology. Universalism denied a limited atonement and election to condemnation and punishment. John Murray (1741-1815), who had been associated with Whitefield's tabernacle in London, came to Massachusetts in 1770 and by 1779 organized a congregation at Gloucester along Universalist lines.[3] Elhanan Winchester, a Baptist minister, founded a Baptist Universalist society in 1785. A convention of all Universalists in America in 1790 in Philadelphia brought into being a national organization with a statement of faith. Hosea Ballou (1771-1852) was the theologian of Universalism and expressed his ideas in his *Treatise on the Atonement* (1805). Denial of any future punishment and final salvation for all is the major tenet of the group, although in many respects there is a close affinity with Unitarianism. Both denominations voted in 1960 to unite their forces.

King's Chapel, the first Episcopal church in New England, under the leadership of James Freeman (1759-1835), a lay reader who was finally ordained by the congregation in 1785, took all mention of the Trinity out of the order of worship. It became the first Unitarian church in this country. When Henry Ware became professor of theology at Harvard in 1805, the Unitarian forces gained another victory, but the conservative forces established Andover Seminary in 1808 to uphold orthodoxy.

[3] *Ibid.,* pp. 399, 400.

William Ellery Channing (1780-1842), a graduate of Harvard and minister of the Federal Street Church in Boston, gave classic expression to Unitarian theology in his sermon in Baltimore in 1819 at the ordination of Jared Sparks.[4] He exalted reason and rejected the Trinity in favor of the unity of God. In addition, he rejected the deity of Christ, whom he made to be distinct from God and like man, who was basically good. The divine spark within responsible able man would enable him to secure his salvation by his own efforts.

This credo of Unitarianism was followed in 1825 by the union of about one hundred twenty-five former Congregational churches into the American Unitarian Association, with Channing as its first president. Transfer of church property to this organization was aided by the Dedham case in 1820, in which the Supreme Court of Massachusetts decided that church property belonged to all the voters of the parish rather than to the communicants who regularly attended church. Thus the voters had a right to choose the minister and to dispose of the property in spite of the desire of the communicant members. About eighty churches were transferred to Unitarianism as a result of this decision. The intellectual, fashionable and rich elite of New England Congregationalism went over to Unitarianism. Thus Puritan New England of Calvinistic persuasion became largely Unitarian New England after the Dedham decision of 1820 and the rupture of 1825.

Many Quakers in urban areas had accepted the full authority of the Bible and the doctrine of human depravity in opposition to the Quaker dogma of the inner light as the main source of revelation. Elias Hicks (1748-1830) made the inner light the final authority and held to the Pelagian idea that each person was a sinner by choice and not by birth. This led him to deny the substitutionary atonement of Christ. In 1827 he and his followers withdrew from the Philadelphia Yearly Meeting to found their own meeting, and others in New York, Ohio, Indiana and Baltimore followed suit until about half of the Quakers were in the Hicksite camp.

An Arminian Baptist group, the Freewill Baptists, came into being in New England in 1780 under the leadership of Benjamin Randall, a former Congregationalist. A General Conference was organized in 1820, and the denomination grew rapidly. Even earlier, in 1727, an Arminian Baptist group had been organized in the South by Paul Palmer.

[4]*Ibid.*, pp. 404-407.

Both in the East and West disagreements over theology, revivalism and church practice had brought into being many new denominations. This tendency to schism and the formation of new churches was not to be arrested until the development of the ecumenical movement in the late nineteenth and early twentieth centuries.

BIBLIOGRAPHY

FORBUSH, BLISS. *Elias Hicks, Quaker Liberal.* New York: Columbia University Press, 1956. Interesting biography based on sources.

GARRISON, WINFRED E., and DEGROOT, ALFRED T. *The Disciples of Christ, A History* (rev.). St. Louis: Bethany Press, 1958. An able history of Campbell's and Stone's movements.

KROMMINGA, JOHN H. *The Christian Reformed Church.* Grand Rapids: Baker Book House, 1949.

OLMSTEAD. *HRUS.* Pp. 236, 237, 295-310.

SWEET. *SRA.* Pp. 231-242.

WILBUR, EARL M. *A History of Unitarianism.* Cambridge: Harvard University Press, 1946.

12

FULFILLING THE GREAT COMMISSION

EVEN THOUGH THE RESULTS of the War of 1812 had been inconclusive, that war had stimulated the spirit of nationalism which had been originally fostered by the Revolutionary War and the adoption of the Constitution. The movement of the population to the West challenged religious forces to meet the religious needs of the rapidly growing frontier society. The dilution of Calvinism by liberal thinkers, with their emphasis upon human responsibility and the dignity of man, made it necessary to give men religious and educational opportunity whether they were living in the East or West. This brought the need for missions, educational institutions and literature to the fore. The first quarter of the nineteenth century saw great strides by the church in these areas.

Missionary Activity of the Church

In many respects the missionary movement in America was a part of the great missionary movement of the nineteenth century, which Kenneth S. Latourette designates as "the great century" in missions among Protestants. It followed and was largely inspired by the wave of late eighteenth century revival, which brought the Evangelical Awakening in the Church of England in England and the Second Awakening in America. It will be remembered that Carey went to India in 1792 and Judson went to that same land in 1812.

Home Missions. Both home and foreign missions usually began as local interdenominational activities and then became denominational in scope. Missionary activity was not confined to the white settlers in the West but was also extended to Indians and Negroes.

The New York Missionary Society included Presbyterian, Baptist and Dutch Reformed people among its supporters at the time of its founding in 1796 to carry the gospel to the Indians. The American Home Missionary Society of 1826 was in one sense an extension of the Plan of Union between Congregationalists and Presbyterians and sought to organize churches and serve the settlers who had moved to the West. Its missionaries preferred to work in the area north of the slave-holding states because they came from the Northeast. In 1828 an "Illinois Band" of eleven students at Yale was organized to serve as teachers and ministers in Illinois. Some of them were instrumental in the founding of Illinois College. Another group of eleven men from Andover went to Iowa in 1843, and some of them helped to found Iowa College (Grinnell). Stephen Peet helped to found Beloit College and Chicago Theological Seminary. Both spiritual and educational needs were met. By the middle of the nineteenth century the society had more than one thousand missionaries in the West.

Denominational groups also founded denominational societies. The Missionary Society of Connecticut was founded by the Congregationalists in 1798 to meet the needs of settlers and the Indians. David Bacon, its first missionary, was sent to the area of Lake Erie in 1800. *The Connecticut Evangelical Magazine* began publication in 1800 to spread missionary propaganda to stimulate missionary activity. Other societies later followed with their own missionary publications. The Presbyterians in 1802 appointed a committee to promote missions. This committee became the Board of Missions in 1816 and subsidized churches in the West so that they might have their own pastors. The Baptists of Massachusetts founded their Missionary Society in 1802, and the Methodists organized their missionary work under the Methodist Missionary Society in 1819 as a result of the work of James Stewart among the Indians in Ohio.

Ministry to the Indians as well as the white settlers was a part of the work of these societies. Isaac McCoy (1784-1846) was instrumental in the opening of Baptist work among the Indians in the area of present Indiana and Michigan and began a school at Fort Wayne in 1820. In 1834 Jason Lee (1803-1845) was sent to the Willamette Valley by the Methodists and ministered to both Indians and the settlers. Dr. Marcus Whitman and his wife and a minister named Henry Spaulding and his wife, all of whom were Presbyterians, went to the Oregon Territory in 1836 to evangelize the Indians and help them improve their agriculture. Whitman alerted the country to the value of the area and led settlers there in 1843. Suspecting that the missionaries were responsible for epidemics, Indians massacred the Whitmans and twelve others in 1847. Work among the Indians by missionaries of other denominations soon followed these pioneering efforts.

Missionary work with the Negroes was not neglected by the churches. The Methodists began work among the slaves in 1787, and by 1815 had nearly one hundred missionaries engaged in that type of endeavor. Many of the best missionaries were recruited from the Negro population. This activity soon led to the formation of Negro denominations. In 1792 the Bethel African Methodist Episcopal Church was organized by a Negro named Richard Allen. This proliferation of denominations among the Negroes has gone on steadily since that time, but particularly after the Civil War, when former slaves wanted to cut all connections with their former masters.

Foreign Missions. Reports of the work of missionaries such as William Carey from England, the acquisition of California and consequent enlarged contact with the Far East brought about interest in foreign missions. Samuel Mills (1783-1818) and several students at Williams College, in a prayer meeting by a haystack during a storm, pledged themselves in 1806 to do foreign missionary work. They were joined by Adoniram Judson (1788-1850) when they went to Andover Seminary. This group in 1810 petitioned[1] the Congregational Association of Massachusetts to found a foreign missionary society and to use them as the first missionaries. The American Board of Commissioners for Foreign Missions came into being that year, and in 1812 Presbyterians and later Dutch Reformed ministers were added to the board so that it became interdenominational.

Judson and several others set sail for India in 1812, but en route Judson and Luther Rice became convinced by the study of the Bible that immersion was the correct mode of baptism. They therefore were immersed in Carey's church in Calcutta. Rice returned to America and Judson, who was not allowed to remain in India, went to Burma where he won more than seven thousand converts, translated the Bible into Burmese and compiled an English-Burmese dictionary. This was in addition to being largely responsible for the founding of the first American foreign missionary society. This society also undertook work in Hawaii, now a state, and won many in the islands to Christianity. The

[1]Peter G. Mode, *Sourcebook and Bibliographical Guide to American Church History* (Menasha, Wis.: George Banta Publishing Co., 1921), p. 371.

leading families in the islands are descendants of these early Congregational missionaries, and Congregationalism is still important in Hawaiian religious life. Later, Chinese and Japanese immigration to Hawaii resulted in the introduction of Buddhism and Shintoism.

The return of Judson's colleague Rice to America and their conversion to Baptist principles challenged the Baptists of America to missionary activity, and in 1814 a Baptist missionary society was organized. This constituted the first united national organization of Baptists and began the formation of denominational missionary societies.

After a period of cooperation with the ABCFM, Presbyterians and the Dutch Reformed founded the United Foreign Missionary Society in 1817, which lasted until 1825. The Old School Presbyterians organized a denominational Board of Missions in 1837. Other denominations did the same even before this time.

Opposition to missionary work either at home or abroad developed in the West, particularly among the Baptists under the leadership of John Taylor and Alexander Campbell. Taylor's pamphlet *Thoughts on Missions* (1819) summarized some of the objections. Adherence to a rigid Calvinism, which meant that God would save the elect without human help, made missions unnecessary. Many who adhered to a loose democratic polity were opposed to rigid centralized organizations and authority. The missionary with superior education and a regular stipend was often an object of suspicion to the poorly educated or uneducated settler. In spite of such opposition, both home and foreign missions expanded rapidly.

The Church Promotes Education

The passion for learning was not neglected by the churches. Educational activity developed on all levels. The Sunday school, which Robert Raikes, a journalist in Gloucester, England, had popularized in his newspaper in 1780, soon emerged on the American religious scene. William Elliott founded one in Virginia in 1785, and the Methodists soon took up this technique of religious education. By 1790 the movement spread to Philadelphia. Need of a national organization was soon apparent, and in 1824 the American Sunday-School Union was founded to promote Sunday schools and to provide literature for those already in existence. Denominations also organized departments to promote that work in their own churches.

Before 1825 education had been in the hands of private groups or, as in New England, where the church had been endowed, in publicly supported institutions of a religious nature. The movement toward the secularization of public education got under way after 1825 through the work of Horace Mann (1796-1859), who promoted tax-supported compulsory secular schools. He was not averse to nonsectarian instruction in biblical doctrine and ethics. Many clergymen opposed this secular system and preferred parochial schools. But only the Lutherans and Roman Catholics have consistently held to this position, and the private and parochial school movement still seems to be growing.

The founding of educational institutions was aided by the Dartmouth College case (1819), in which the decision permitted colleges to remain independent of state control after they were chartered.[2] Land speculators in the West offered land grants to colleges in the hope that the presence of such an institution in a new town would encourage settlement and give them profits from the sale of land. Some schools were founded to meet the need for ministerial candidates to staff the increasing number of churches. Soon all the denominations sponsored the establishment and development of colleges in the West.

Presbyterians early established colleges in the West. Most of these had a predominance of ministers on their faculty. Transylvania College was founded in 1783, but did not open its doors until two years later. Blount College, which was to become the University of Tennessee, began operations in 1794. Other Presbyterian colleges included Wabash, Washington and Jefferson, and Davidson. The Congregationalists established Marietta in 1790, Amherst (Illinois), and Iowa College, later to be known as Grinnell. The Baptists founded Colby in 1820 in Maine, and Shurtleff in Illinois through the efforts of John M. Peck. The Methodists began to establish colleges in the 1830's. The founding of Wesleyan University in Connecticut in 1831 was soon followed by Randolph-Macon, McKendree (Illinois), Emory and DePauw.

Theological seminaries were also established in large numbers to meet the need for ministers to take care of the growing population, particularly those who were won to the church in revivals. As early as 1784 the Dutch Reformed initiated efforts which eventuated in New Brunswick Theological Seminary in 1810. Andover

[2]Henry S. Commager (ed.), *Documents of American History* (4th ed.; New York: Appleton-Century-Crofts, Inc., 1948), pp. 220-223.

Seminary was founded in 1807 because of the defection of Harvard to Unitarianism. Bangor Seminary in Maine was started in 1816. Both were the work of Congregationalists. The Presbyterians launched Princeton Seminary in 1812 and a few years later Auburn and Union (Richmond, Virginia) Seminaries. The Baptists established Newton Theological Seminary in Massachusetts in 1825. The Episcopalians brought General Theological Seminary into being, and the Lutherans founded the Lutheran Seminary at Gettysburg in this same period. By 1840 about twenty-five seminaries had been opened.

The need of Bibles on the frontier was pointed out by Samuel Mills after tours of the West between 1812 and 1815, and the American Bible Society was founded in 1816 in New York to supplement the work of earlier state societies. It did a splendid job in providing Bibles for those in need of them.

The American Tract Society came into being in 1825, also in New York, to create literature which would promote evangelical ideas throughout the country.[3] Devotional literature, histories, biographies, and tracts poured out of its offices in great quantities.

Missionary and religious magazines were printed in large numbers to bring the message of missions into homes. As early as 1800 the missionary organization of the Congregationalists in Connecticut founded the *Connecticut Evangelical Magazine* to promote the work of that society. Other societies of this and other denominations soon followed. The Methodists began the Methodist Book Concern in 1789 in New York, the first such denominational press, and established the *Methodist Magazine* in 1818. Other denominations soon set up denominational presses and magazines.

This voluntary outpouring of religious energy in home and foreign missions, Sunday schools, colleges, seminaries, religious presses and magazines and literature societies helped to meet the needs of the growing western population. Without such efforts the western settlers might not have made the rapid cultural progress they did make.

BIBLIOGRAPHY

ANDERSON, COURTNEY. *To the Golden Shore: The Life of Adoniram Judson.* Boston: Little, Brown and Co., 1956. A popular but scholarly biography.

[3]Mode, *op. cit.*, pp. 383, 384.

OLMSTEAD. *HRUS*. Pp. 265-294.

SWEET. *SRA*. Pp. 243-257, 309, 310.

TEWKSBURY, DONALD G. *The Founding of American Colleges and Universities Before the Civil War*. New York: Teachers College, Columbia University Press, 1932.

WAYLAND, FRANCIS. *A Memoir of the Life and Labors of Adoniram Judson*. Boston: Phillips, Sampson and Co., 1853. A good account with much useful source material.

13

CONFLICTS IN THEOLOGY
AND POLITY

THE NATIONALISTIC SPIRIT, which had been prominent even in the field of religion, gave way between 1828 and 1865 to sectionalism and schism in religion. The slavery controversy, the freedom of the frontier, and immigration, particularly that of the Irish and Germans, brought on tensions over polity and theology which either resulted in the formation of new denominations or in hostile parties coexisting within a denomination. The present chapter will illustrate this pattern.

Controversy and Schism or Intradenominational Parties

The first denomination to be rent by differences over theology and, to a lesser extent, polity was the Presbyterian. In his sermon at the Yale commencement in 1828, Nathaniel Taylor had asserted that while man has sinful inclinations he is not totally depraved. Self-love, the desire for happiness, would promote the regenerative process. This sermon angered many Presbyterians. In 1829 Albert Barnes preached the sermon "Way of Salvation" before his Presbyterian congregation in Morristown, New Jersey, in which he denied that Adam's descendants inherited his guilt. Efforts to remove him from his position in Morristown and later from his larger church in Philadelphia were unsuccessful both in the local presbytery and the General Assembly of the church. Lyman Beecher (1775-1863), talented president of Lane Theological Seminary in Cincinnati, Ohio, was charged with heresy before the presbytery by Joshua Wilson for his views on original sin, but he was acquitted. The more liberal forces poured still more oil on the fire in 1836 by founding the independent Union Seminary in New York.

Doctrinal tension was heightened by strain over the question of slavery. Although the Old School group had antislavery supporters, the strength of the antislavery force was in the New School wing of Presbyterians. Thus if the New School men had been allowed to discuss slavery in the General Assembly it might have divided the Old School group. For that reason the issue was kept in the background as much as possible.

The New School group tended to favor the Plan of Union of 1801, but the Old School group increasingly came to oppose it because of the manner in which it diluted strong control of the churches by the presbyteries. In the General Assembly of 1837, men of the Old School, who were in the majority, ended the Plan of Union, created a separate Board of Foreign Missions and forced the New School men out of the church. Not until 1852 in the Albany Convention did the Congregationalists disavow the plan and seek to win the West for Congregationalism.

The New School Presbyterian church was founded in 1838 with almost half the Presbyterian church in it. Its strength was mainly in the North. The Old School under the theological leadership of Charles Hodge (1797-1878), the writer of a noted work on theology, had more than one hundred twenty-five thousand members. Not until 1869 did the Old School and New School in the North reunite their forces, but in the South they reunited in 1864.

While the Episcopal church was able to avoid division, divergent tendencies within that group created intradenominational parties. Bishop John H. Hobart (1775-1830) became the leader of a High Church group which opposed interdenominational cooperation, the doctrine of total depravity and election to condemnation, but emphasized the sacraments. Bishop Alexander Griswold (1766-1843) led the Low Church forces, which opposed the ritualistic tendencies of their opponents. These tendencies had been imported from England by those sympathetic with the Oxford movement, which had created similar divisions in the Church of England. Some of the High Church clergymen went over to the Roman Catholic church. The cleavage was apparent by 1835, but the Anglo-Catholic or High Church party and the Low Church group did not split, largely through the efforts of William Muhlenberg, grandson of the first Muhlenberg. Thus the two parties remained within the church until 1873. In that year Bishop George Cummins (1822-1876) led a small evangelical group out of the church to found the Reformed Episcopal Church. Its membership centered in New York and Philadelphia.

The German Reformed church faced the problem of the "Mercersburg theology" which came out of Mercersburg Theological

Seminary. John W. Nevin (1803-1886) was the main exponent of these ideas of the importance of Christ's person in salvation and His spiritual presence in the communion. Influenced by Friedrich Schleiermacher, they thought that experience was more important than doctrine.

Philip Schaff (1819-1893), who was also of this persuasion, became the leading American church historian by the production of his multivolume history of the church to the end of the Reformation, and by the editing with others or by himself of multivolume sets of the writings of the church fathers. He was also the influential chairman of the committee which produced the American Revised Version of the Bible. Mention should also be made of his contributions to the early ecumenical movement.

Between 1840 and 1860 the Jewish population in the United States multiplied tenfold. Liberalism in Protestantism began to make its influence felt in Judaism, and Reform Judaism emerged in this period under the leadership of Isaac M. Wise (1819-1900). This new Jewish group was much more liberal than the Orthodox Jews. It rejected much of the ceremonial law and rites and gave up the idea of a coming Messiah in an attempt to accommodate to the surrounding culture.

Immigration and Controversy

Immigration also created problems in this period because those whose families had been in the United States for several generations found their ideas clashing with those of the later arrivals who came in great numbers from Ireland and Germany. By 1860 nearly one-eighth of the population or more than four million people in the United States had been born abroad. Over one million six hundred thousand Irish came to the United States between 1841 and 1855 because of exploitation by absentee English landlords. The forced payment of tithes to maintain the Anglican church in a predominantly Roman Catholic Ireland had angered them. A blight on the potato crop in 1845 brought starvation in Ireland. The failure of the democratic revolution in 1848 and consequent persecution forced many Germans, such as the soon famous Carl Schurz, to migrate to the United States. By 1861 more than one million three hundred thousand had migrated to this country. Linguistic and theological problems created tension between the newcomers and those already here in both the Roman Catholic and Lutheran churches.

Bishop John Hughes (1797-1864) of New York became the

storm center in the Roman Catholic church around which the problems of parochial schools and "trusteeism" centered. The problem of educating the many Roman Catholic Irish migrants who had come to New York had to be decided. Should public schools carry on that task, or should the church establish parochial schools? Hughes opposed public education and developed in New York a parochial system which became the model for other areas of the church. Teaching orders of nuns, such as Elizabeth Seton's Sisters of Charity, were organized and took over the task of staffing the parochial schools. Higher education was mainly in the hands of the Jesuit order after its revival in 1814.

The problem of trusteeism arose because many states permitted local congregations to form corporations which would hold property. Many Roman Catholic congregations wanted to avail themselves of this right, but the hierarchy opposed them. An organization of Roman Catholic trustees was incorporated in New York City to buy land and to build a church. This group also claimed it could appoint and dismiss their pastors. Bishop Hughes was finally able to secure control of the property for the bishop and to have the choice of pastors left to the bishop.

Nationalist opposition by Protestants was another problem. Protestants became alarmed over the danger of a growing Roman Catholicism to which the publicity about trusteeship and parochial school disputes called attention. About 1840 Bishop Hughes's campaign in New York City and in Albany before the state legislature for the extension of public aid from tax money to parochial schools alarmed the country. In addition, the work of missionary orders in the West, which was successful in winning many to Catholicism, frightened Protestants. Books, such as Maria Monk's *Awful Disclosures,* with tales of immorality between priests and nuns, and Lyman Beecher's sermons against Romanism, aggravated tension.

To combat the forces of Roman Catholicism to which immigration was adding its millions, the Native American party was founded in 1837 to limit immigration and to increase the time necessary before one could apply for naturalization papers. The Know-Nothing movement became a secret organization in 1850 and dedicated itself to opposition to the Roman Catholic church. It won control of nine state legislatures and elected about seventy-five congressmen in the 1854 election. Millard Fillmore was its candidate for the presidency. Fortunately for the Roman Catholic church, the rising slavery issue distracted public attention from the church until the 1880's, when the American Protective Association was founded to protect America from supposed foreign religious control.

Large numbers of German Lutheran immigrants arrived after 1848, and in the 1850's nearly seventy-five thousand Scandinavian Lutheran immigrants created further problems for the Lutherans in the United States, who were already facing controversy. The American Lutherans, led by Samuel Schmucker (1799-1873), a professor at Gettysburg Seminary, in order to unite all Lutherans in America, wanted to interpret the Augsburg Confession more liberally and to use English in the services of the church. The confessional party wanted strict adherence to the Augsburg Confession and the exclusive use of German in the services of the church. This attempt to Americanize Lutheranism was defeated by the large German immigration after 1848.

Nationalism among the new German Lutheran immigrants led to the formation of new conservative Lutheran denominations. Carl F. W. Walther (1811-1887) became leader of a group which in Saxony had opposed the growing liberalism in the Lutheran church and had finally migrated to the United States to settle around St. Louis. Partly through his German paper *Der Lutheraner,* which he began in 1844, he was able by 1847 to organize in Chicago the Missouri Synod as it is now popularly known. It soon became one of the main Lutheran bodies. Other German groups organized the Buffalo (1845) and Iowa (1854) Synods.

Scandinavian Lutheran migration brought still other national Lutheran churches into being. Norwegian Lutherans united in 1853 in the Synod of the Norwegian Evangelical Lutheran Church. The Swedish Lutherans in 1860 founded the Augustana Synod, with a college at Rock Island, Illinois. Nationalism has been the major reason for the large number of Lutheran denominations in this land. Only lately have they begun to reunite in larger churches which are crossing national lines.

BIBLIOGRAPHY

BILLINGTON, RAY A. *Protestant Crusade, 1800-1860.* Gloucester, Mass.: Peter Smith, reprinted 1963.
OLMSTEAD. *HRUS.* Pp. 311-333.
SWEET. *SRA.* Pp. 258-273.

14

CULTIST AND COMMUNAL GROUPS

Up to this point attention has been devoted to what may be described as churches and sects. Churches have a creed and, in colonial days, had an affiliation with the state and practiced infant baptism. Sects repudiate a state church, have no formal confession, look on Christianity as a way of life, and usually emphasize believer baptism. In the first half of the nineteenth century the cult, with its leader and with its religious authority often outside the Scripture, or in the Scripture and another book, emerged. Mormonism and Spiritualism were characteristic of this approach on the frontier, and in the urban environment Christian Science illustrates the same tendency. Most of the American churches and sects were imports from Europe, but the cults to be discussed were indigenous to the United States.

Various causes have promoted the rise of new sects and cults. The freer atmosphere of America and the right of individual interpretation of the Bible which came with the Reformation gave rise to aberrant approaches to religion. Nationality or language, particularly in the case of the Lutheran churches, and racial feeling among the Negroes have promoted the rise of many groups. A communal approach as opposed to private approach to property, as in the case of the Oneida, Shaker and other communities, brought several communal groups into being. Differences concerning the polity of the church were a factor in the rise of other groups. Sectionalism over the slavery issue split many churches into Northern and Southern wings. As already noticed, immigration accounted for many of the diverse groups in colonial America. Revivalism played its part in promoting new groups. At this point, however, attention must be given to the frontier as a fertile field for the emergence of new groups.

Rural New England, Pennsylvania, which was free from a state or privileged church, the old Northwest and particularly western New York, which had recurrent waves of revival accompanied by great emotion, became centers for a number of cults. In western New York, the Millerite movement, Spiritualism, Mormonism and anti-Masonic tendencies as well as the communal Oneida cult originated. This "burned-over district" thus accounts for most of the religious groups described in this chapter.

Particular emphases are prominent in the thinking and literature of such groups. Spiritualism catered to the desire to know something about the destiny of deceased loved ones. Others sought economic security by such positive affirmative beliefs as those of Unity. The desire for health led many to healing cults, such as Christian Science. Interest in the future motivated such groups as those who followed William Miller. Some sought relief from fear of death or future punishment. Others found a sense of belonging in some cults which they were unable to achieve in the old-line denominations. These appeals coupled with a fervent evangelistic zeal have made cults attractive to many people in the United States.

Frontier Cults of Western New York

Mormonism arose in western New York to become in 1830 an organized church through the work of Joseph Smith (1805-1844). His storekeeper parents had migrated to Palmyra from Vermont. They seem to have been visionary individuals, and in 1820 Joseph Smith had his first vision and shortly thereafter confessed conversion. In 1827, supposedly at the command of the angel Moroni, Smith claimed to have dug up in the hill Cumorah golden plates with the story of early American religious history. The warlike Lamanites, or American Indians, fought with the godly Nephites until only a few Nephites were left. Moroni buried the records of the Nephites in the hill from which Smith supposedly obtained them. Smith dictated to his disciples from behind a curtain what was supposed to be on these plates. Thus the *Book of Mormon*, which was published in 1830, came into being during the same year in which Smith and five others formed at Fayette what was to become the Mormon church or, as it is properly called, the Church of Jesus Christ of Latter-Day Saints.

The small group moved to Kirtland, Ohio, in 1831. They remained there until in the Panic of 1837 the failure of the bank which they had set up forced them to migrate from the hostile community. They settled in Independence, Missouri, from 1837 until 1839, when because of their large-scale land purchases hostility again forced them to move. Later, under the leadership of one of Smith's sons, the Reorganized church was to set up its headquarters here and to deny the revelation of polygamy to Joseph Smith. From 1840 to 1844 Smith and his followers were busy organizing a strong Mormon settlement of fifteen thousand on the east bank of the Mississippi at Nauvoo, Illinois. Smith's revelation of polygamy in 1843, which was to provide physical bodies for disembodied spirits brought into being by deity, brought death finally to Smith and his brother at the hands of an angry mob in the jail in which they had been placed. Many Mormons under the leadership of Brigham Young trekked to Utah by 1847, where they founded the state of Deseret at Salt Lake. Large-scale irrigation and community enterprise and co-operation under the vigorous leadership of Young brought prosperity. Their massacre of settlers on their way west in 1857 and federal opposition to polygamy led to a conflict which finally resulted in the creation of the state of Utah in 1896. In both Utah and Southern Idaho the Mormons now form the major part of the church population.

The Mormon church is a highly organized entity with a pyramidal hierarchy of apostles and a priesthood serving under them. Tithing brings much wealth to the community, which uses it to help the needy. The practice of young people giving one to two years of their lives to propaganda abroad has resulted in the worldwide spread of the church.

An interchurch *Adventist* or millennial movement grew out of the millennial teachings of a New England farmer of Baptist persuasion named William Miller (1782-1849). Later followers added the keeping of the Old Testament dietary laws, the seventh day Sabbath, the doctrine of soul sleep between death and the resurrection at the advent of Christ, the final annihilation of the wicked and an imperfect view of Christ's atonement.

Miller moved to New York and served as an army captain in the War of 1812. He became a Baptist and earnestly studied his Bible for many years. His study of the two thousand three hundred days of Daniel 8:14 led him to the idea that a day represented a year. The two thousand three hundred years, which began in 457 B.C., gave a date of 1843 for the second coming of Christ. His lectures led many to adopt his ideas. Great disappointment followed among his followers when Christ did not come in 1843, and it was announced by one of Miller's disciples that He would come in 1844.

The Seventh-Day Adventists emerged from Miller's followers in 1845 and were led by Ellen G. White (1827-1915). The non-appearance of Christ to earth in 1843 and 1844 was explained by the idea that He did come in 1844 to the most holy place in heaven, from whence He will eventually return to earth after He completes the atonement begun at Calvary. This group made Battle Creek, Michigan, their headquarters until 1903, when they moved to Takoma Park, Washington, D.C. Their practice of tithing gives them large sums for their hospitals, publications and missions.

Spiritualism was still another cult which emerged in western New York. The idea of communication with the spirit world was brought to this country by the Swedenborgians. In 1848, Margaret and Kate Fox of Hydesville, New York, began to complain of rapping noises in their room. They supposedly had communication with spirits of the dead. Out of this beginning came a national organization of Spiritualists in 1863. Many prominent individuals were attracted to the group. The desire for contact with dead soldiers by members of their families stimulated the expansion of the group after World War I.

Religious Communal Experiments on the Frontier

Several religious communal cults arose in the United States between the Revolutionary and Civil Wars. The freedom of the frontier provided living room where these groups could try out their experiments in communal living.

Different reasons seem to have motivated the formation of these groups. Some took the voluntary and temporary communal practice of the early church literally as a divine model and sought to found ideal Christian Utopias. People who came from Europe without money for a start in the New World sometimes found communal living to be the answer to their economic problems. Others desired to withdraw from sinful society and to develop a perfect life in combination with others of similar mind. It must be remembered that perfectionism was associated with the preaching of many revivalists in the period before the Civil War. Others felt they could better prepare themselves for Christ's soon coming by separation from society.

An early experiment had been carried out by Conrad Beissel, who left the Dunkers in 1732 and founded the Ephrata Society in Lancaster, Pennsylvania, along communal lines, with opposition to marriage and the observance of the seventh day as the true Sabbath. After the death of Beissel in 1768 the society declined. This movement for a time won many away from the Dunkers.

2.2.125

The Shaker movement, or the Millennial church, had its beginnings in England. Ann Lee (1736-1784), one of eight children of an English blacksmith, married, but the many children of the marriage died in infancy. In 1758, probably as a result of these experiences, she united with a group of Shaking Quakers. She claimed to have visions and spoke in tongues. Mother Lee, as they called her, and several followers migrated in 1774 to New York state, where she later organized a Shaker community. Several communities were founded on the frontier in Ohio, Kentucky and Indiana. Because sex was believed to be the source of all sin, the group adopted celibacy. They substituted the revelations of Ann, who was looked upon as a female Christ, for those in the Bible and rejected the two sacraments. Ritual dancing was used to help them shake out sin. Communal organization would help them remain separated from the world. After the Civil War the movement declined.[1]

John Humphrey Noyes (1811-1886), who had been influenced by Finney and had trained at Dartmouth College, Andover Seminary and Yale Divinity School, began to teach the possibility of sinless perfection here and now. His preaching in 1846 of stirpiculture, the idea that every woman was every man's wife and every man every woman's husband in the group and that sex relations were to be regulated so that only an annual quota of children should be born, created so much opposition to the communal organization which he had set up in Putney, Vermont, in 1843, that he moved the community to Oneida, New York, in 1848. The group began to manufacture superior traps to catch fur-bearing animals. This and the later manufacture of silverware brought them prosperity. By 1880 complex marriage was given up, and the group was reorganized as a joint-stock company, which still manufactures silverware.

George Rapp (1757-1847), a pietistic peasant from Germany, who looked for the imminent return of Christ, came with his followers to Harmony in western Pennsylvania to escape persecution in the homeland and to set up a communal colony there by 1804. They later migrated to Indiana and built New Harmony, which was sold to Robert Owen, the English Utopian socialist, and they returned to Economy in Pennsylvania. The Amana Society was another German group practicing community of prop-

[1]Peter G. Mode, *Sourcebook and Bibliographical Guide to American Church History* (Menasha, Wis.: George Banta Publishing Co., 1921), pp. 353-358.

erty, making its home finally in Amana, Iowa, before the Civil War.

Brook Farm, still another communal experiment, near Boston, was dedicated more to intellectual or cultural pursuits. George Ripley (1802-1880), a Unitarian minister, founded it about the middle of the nineteenth century. Nathaniel Hawthorne and intellectually distinguished transcendentalists participated in it, but the impractical nature of the group kept it from being a success. Hopedale Community, founded by the Universalist minister Hosea Ballou, was a similar experiment to bring the kingdom of God on earth, but it broke up about 1856.

Few of these communal movements remained after the Civil War. Tendencies to reunion of churches, the filling of the frontier by immigration, urbanization, and industrialization made such communal movements difficult to maintain.

BIBLIOGRAPHY

Olmstead. *HRUS*. Pp. 334-346.
Sweet. *SRA*. Pp. 273-283.

General Works on Cults:

Braden, Charles S. *These Also Believe*. New York: The Macmillan Co., 1949. A sympathetic study of several cults based on much research and with extensive bibliography.

Clark, Elmer T. *The Small Sects in America* (2nd ed. rev.). New York: Abingdon-Cokesbury Press, 1949.

Ferguson, Charles W. *The Confusion of Tongues*. Garden City, N.Y.: Doubleday, Doran and Co., 1936. A fairly objective but sometimes cynical history of many of the cults.

Gerstner, John H. *The Theology of the Major Sects*. Grand Rapids: Baker Book House, 1960. An able discussion of the history and doctrine of groups denying evangelical doctrine.

Martin, Walter R. *The Rise of the Cults*. Grand Rapids: Zondervan Publishing House, 1955.

Van Baalen, Jan K. *The Chaos of Cults* (2nd ed. rev. and enl.). Grand Rapids: Wm. B. Eerdmans Publishing Co., 1956. A standard study of the history and doctrines of the major cults contrasted with the biblical doctrines.

Mormonism:

Brodie, Fawn M. *No Man Knows My History*. New York: Alfred A. Knopf, 1945. The life story of Joseph Smith.

Linn, William A. *The Story of the Mormons*. New York: The Macmillan Co., 1902. An able history.

Adventism:

SEARS, CLARA E. *Days of Delusion.* Boston: Houghton Mifflin Co., 1924. A critical account of Miller and his followers.

Communal Cults:

MADISON, CHARLES A. *Critics and Crusaders.* New York: Frederick Ungar Publishing Co., 1959.

TYLER, ALICE F. *Freedom's Ferment.* Minneapolis: University of Minnesota Press, 1944.

WEBBER, EVERETT. *Escape to Utopia: The Communal Movement in America.* New York: Hastings House Publishers, 1959.

Able accounts of American communal groups in the last three books.

15

REVIVALISM AND PERFECTIONISM

Between the Second Awakening and the beginning of the Civil War the major revival movements were associated with the name of Charles Finney and the lay revival of 1857-1858. Other evangelists, such as Asahel Nettleton before Finney and after him Jacob Knapp among the Baptists, were secondary stars. This revivalism, as Timothy Smith has demonstrated so ably in his *Revivalism and Social Reform in Mid-Nineteenth Century America*, promoted both personal and social perfectionist tendencies among its converts. Perhaps the optimism after the Civil War also provided a favorable climate of opinion for an evangelical postmillennial social perfectionism that was eventually to contribute to the rise of the Social Gospel.

Revivalism in the Eastern United States

Charles G. Finney (1792-1875) was a lawyer who lived in the "burned-over district" in western New York. He was converted in 1821, began independent theological study and then entered the Presbyterian ministry. Doubts about the Calvinistic doctrine of election and limited atonement and his perfectionist tendencies brought about his transfer to Congregationalism.

He became a successful evangelist and from 1826 conducted large meetings in such cities as Philadelphia, New York and Boston. The Rochester meeting in 1831, where he first used the "anxious bench," was one of his most fruitful with at least one thousand converts of whom forty entered the ministry. Estimates of his converts ran as high as one hundred thousand. He introduced such "new measures" as the anxious bench at the front of the auditorium for those concerned about their souls, and cottage prayer meetings where women were allowed to participate and people would be prayed for by name. In 1834 and 1835 Finney settled down briefly as pastor in New York's Broadway Tabernacle, which had been built for him by the wealthy Lewis Tappan. An invitation to become the first professor of theology at Oberlin in 1835 appealed to him as an opportunity to propagate his perfectionist ideas. Even though busy as president of Oberlin from 1851 to 1866, he periodically engaged in revival campaigns. His new measures, his large urban revival campaigns and his *Lectures on Revival* have greatly influenced subsequent revivalism. Finney's work at Oberlin College, where his perfectionist ideas led him to promote social reforms—particularly opposition to slavery—constituted another area of important influence radiating from his life.

Another major revival grew out of the Fulton Street noonday prayer meeting in New York. It began Wednesday, September 23, 1857, as an interdenominational prayer meeting with six present. The revival was a lay movement energized by prayer rather than by preaching, and spread by personal work of individuals rather than by sermons of a great evangelist. A Dutch Reformed Church congregation became concerned about the decline in numbers in their inner city church. They engaged Jeremiah C. Lanphier as a lay missionary. Inspired to meet the spiritual needs growing out of the Panic of 1857, the growing slavery crisis and the large immigration of Irish and Germans, he began his noonday prayer meetings. By October, 1857, forty were in attendance, and by the spring of 1858 there were twenty such meetings. Similar prayer meetings were conducted in Boston, Philadelphia and Chicago.

Estimates of the converts from these prayer meetings run from three hundred thousand to over one million added to the churches. The latter figure seems to be a fair estimate. A former boxer by the name of Gardner was converted and his testimony in Sing Sing was the means of converting Jerry McAuley, who later founded a mission in New York to meet the needs of down-and-out men.

Interdenominational cooperation was also a prominent feature of this prayer meeting revival. The absence of any prominent evangelist or organizer is unique in the history of American evangelism. The burden was carried mainly by lay people. It is interesting that this revival came in the North just before the Civil War, and that in 1863 to 1864 there was a major revival in the Confederate armies of the South.

Personal and Social Perfectionism

An emphasis upon the possibility of perfection of personal and social life seemed to be an outgrowth of the revivals between

1828 and 1858. Perhaps the optimism of an expanding America had something to do with this, but its roots seem to have been primarily theological and historical.

Personal perfection became a matter of interest and teaching about the middle of the century. This teaching suggested the possibility that the individual might be freed from sin in this life and live a sinless life. John Wesley had taught in his little book *Christian Perfection* that it was possible to have the love of God so fill the life that one would not consciously sin even though "mistakes" might still be made. The idea that perfection was possible in this life seems to have been a part of Finney's teaching after he became professor of theology at Oberlin Seminary. With later Holiness groups it became the idea of a second work of grace, subsequent to salvation, that would lead to the entire eradication of sin in the life of the believer. American Methodism, particularly through the work of Phoebe Palmer, came under the influence of the idea that the individual might lead a personal holy life free from sin.

The idea of social perfection seems to have come out of the postmillennial but evangelical revivalism of the era. Through the social activities of Christians it was believed that the nation might be won to God and a veritable kingdom of God be set up on earth by the church. This conception resulted in activities to curb sin in society and to bring in a more perfect social order in which earth might become the kingdom of God. The movement was more pronounced in urban than in rural areas. Social reform also went hand in hand with the work of the great revivalists of the era, many of whom leaned to Arminian theology. As time went on, the emphasis changed from reform through the work of converted individuals to reform by needed social legislation brought about by pressures from interested Christian groups. This technique was suggested by Stephen Colwell in his *New Themes for the Protestant Clergy* (1851).

Liquor was one of the first social abuses to come under attack, although in colonial times on the frontier it had been accepted as a desirable way to convert bulky grain to easily portable goods, which too often the producer himself had sampled heavily. Benjamin Rush in 1784 was the first to point out the effects of alcohol upon mind and body, and soon local and state societies to promote temperance sprang up. By 1836 two nationwide organizations merged to form the American Temperance Union. In 1840, the Washington Temperance Society was the first to be founded on a total abstinence basis, and its members made efforts to re-claim drunkards. Local option laws and state prohibition, first enacted in Maine in 1851, followed.

Dueling was another social evil which religious social reformers attacked, particularly through the preaching of Lyman Beecher. By the beginning of the Civil War the practice had been out-lawed by legislation in many states.

The origins of the peace movement before World War I are to be found in this period. William Ladd was able to get state organizations to unite in the American Peace Society in 1828. He and others then worked on the organization of international peace societies.

Organizations to help wayward girls were set up by church groups. Efforts were made for the provision of Bibles and services for those in prison. Zealous churchmen also carried on antislavery activities to ameliorate its evils and to promote voluntary eman-cipation.

All of these activities helped to strengthen the position of the laity and to give women a more important place in the church and in the reformation of society.

BIBLIOGRAPHY

Olmstead. *HRUS.* Pp. 310, 311, 347-361.
Sweet. *SRA.* Pp. 283, 284, 310, 311.

The Finney Revival:

Cross, Whitney R. *The Burned-Over District.* Ithaca, N.Y.: Cornell University Press, 1950. An able discussion of religion on the New York frontier between 1825 and 1850.

Finney, Charles G. *Lectures on Revivals of Religion.* Boston: John P. Jewett and Co., 1851.

———. *The Memoirs of Rev. Charles G. Finney.* New York: A. S. Barnes and Co., 1876. The evangelist's interpretation of himself.

Wright, George F. *Charles Grandison Finney.* Boston: Houghton Mifflin Co., 1891. A scholarly account.

Revival and Social Reform:

Cole, Charles C., Jr. *The Social Ideas of the Northern Evangelists, 1826-1860.* New York: Columbia University Press, 1954. An able discussion of the ideas and their impact.

Smith, Timothy L. *Revivalism and Social Reform in Mid-Nineteenth Century America.* New York: Abingdon Press, 1957. The linkage of the evangelists' postmillennial interest in social change and re-form with the rise of the Social Gospel.

16

SLAVERY AND SCHISM

EARLY IN THE SEVENTEENTH CENTURY, slavery was introduced into the southern colonies. The institution stimulated the production of tobacco and later indigo in Georgia, rice in South Carolina and especially cotton in the Old South. The aristocratic social structure in the South came to be dependent upon a slave-based economy. Rhode Island, surprisingly enough, was the major center of the trade in New England because the Yankee slave traders found large profits in the lucrative business of supplying slaves to the Southern plantations.

Both in England and in America movements sprang up to bring about the end of the trade and ownership of slaves. Slavery was ended in British possessions by legislative action, but war was to be the final arbiter in bringing about its downfall in America. Perhaps this was due to the fact that, except in the Caribbean, British slavery was more often domestic than field slavery. In both countries the religious forces were important factors in the attempt to deal with this social evil, the first major issue in social morality to occupy the attention of the churches.

Antislavery Activities 1619-1830

The humanitarianism inherent in the early revivals, the deistic interest in man and natural rights philosophy all played a part in the development of means to deal with slavery. Samuel Hopkins (1721-1803), a Congregational minister in Newport, Rhode Island, preached against the slave trade in 1770, and found to his surprise that even those in his congregation engaged in the trade supported him in his efforts to promote voluntary emancipation. He asked the second Continental Congress in 1776 to act against slavery.

Prior to the Revolution the Quakers had been leaders both in England and America in this movement to bring about the gradual end of slavery. George Fox, in his visit to the colonies in 1672 to 1673, had asked the Friends to treat their slaves mildly.

James Keith[1] in 1693 proposed that since Christ had died for all men, including the colored, Christians should not buy slaves and should voluntarily free those whom they might already own. John Woolman, who traveled extensively in the colonies between 1746 and 1772 urging voluntary emancipation of their slaves upon the Friends, recounts the story of his efforts in his *Journal*. It was Anthony Benezet, a Huguenot migrant who taught in Philadelphia, whose books led Wesley to see the evils of the system and to oppose it so strongly. After 1784 Quakers could not belong to monthly meetings if they owned slaves.

Other religious bodies took national or local action after the Revolution. The Methodists, at the meeting in Baltimore in 1784 when the national church was organized, voted to expel members who persisted in the buying and selling of slaves; but this was not consistently enforced. Baptists and Presbyterians also passed resolutions or took action against slavery and the slave trade. The Presbyterian General Assembly in 1818 stated that slavery was a violation of the rights of man and inconsistent with Christianity, and urged its abolition.

After the Revolution began, several of the New England and middle states abolished slavery or provided for its gradual disappearance. The Northwest Ordinance of 1787 banned slavery in territories covered by that ordinance, and the federal Constitution provided that after 1808 no more slaves should be imported.

The first local antislavery society was founded in Philadelphia in 1775 with Benjamin Franklin as its president. Its function was to aid freed Negroes, but it became an abolition society by reorganization in 1787. Similar societies were founded in both Northern and Southern states, and the movement became national in scope with the organization in 1794 of a national society to promote abolition and help the Negro.

There were about two hundred thousand free Negroes in the United States by 1815. As early as 1776 Samuel Hopkins had suggested a plan to set up a colony for them in Africa where they might migrate. The English had started Sierra Leone as a colony for the fourteen thousand slaves freed by judicial action secured through the efforts of Granville Sharp in 1772. The American Colonization Society to colonize the freed slaves in Africa was founded in the beginning of 1817. This society between 1817 and 1867 helped about thirteen thousand Negroes get to Liberia

[1]Peter G. Mode, *Sourcebook and Bibliographical Guide to American Church History* (Menasha, Wis.: George Banta Publishing Co., 1921), pp. 554, 555.

and was thus responsible for what became the Liberian republic in 1847. The amelioration of slavery, gradual emancipation and colonization of freed slaves in Africa dominated the thinking in America until 1830.

Immediate Abolition Demanded 1831-1861

It seemed that slavery might gradually die out until the increased demand for cotton for the mills of Manchester, the invention of Eli Whitney's cotton gin in 1792 and the expansion of the cotton plantations to the rich soil of the new Southwest in Kentucky, Alabama and Mississippi all began to make this main staple of the South immensely profitable. From 1800 to 1860 the number of slaves more than quadrupled to four million, and cotton came to make up over half of American exports. Consequently the price of a good slave rose to two thousand dollars in 1860, whereas it had been only about three hundred dollars in 1790. Cotton was king and created a vested interest, and the South determined to continue slavery. Ministers in the South drew upon the Scriptures for defense of the institution when it came under attack from the aggressive Northern propagandists who demanded immediate abolition.

William Lloyd Garrison (1805-1879) became the leading antislavery agitator in New England in 1830 and began on January 1, 1831, the publication of his paper, the *Liberator*,[2] in which he demanded immediate abolition because slavery was a sin. Those who supported his ideas formed the American Anti-Slavery Society at Philadelphia in 1833.[3] It was dedicated to immediate emancipation. By 1838 more than one thousand auxiliary organizations were bombarding Congress with memorials in favor of the abolition of interstate slave trade. These societies won many supporters from those revivalists and their supporters who were interested in social perfectionism by social reform.

Ohio also became a leading center of agitation against slavery mainly because of the activities of Theodore Dwight Weld (1803-1895). Finney's preaching had led Weld to become a minister. In 1833 Weld moved to Lane Seminary in Cincinnati, where students provided the Negroes of the area with schools and Sunday schools. The trustees and President Lyman Beecher banned the doings of Weld and his followers. In 1834 nearly one hundred students withdrew from the seminary and went to Oberlin Semi-

[2]Henry S. Commager (ed.), *Documents of American History* (4th ed.; New York: Appleton-Century-Crofts, Inc., 1948), pp. 277, 278.
[3]*Ibid.*, pp. 278-281.

nary in 1835 to study under Finney, Asa Mahan (one of the trustees who went with them and became president), and another Lane professor, John Morgan. Oberlin came to be looked upon as the chief center of abolitionism and of the "Oberlin School" theology.

Weld was subsidized by the wealthy Tappan brothers as an agent of the American Anti-Slavery Society after 1835 and is credited with winning Edwin Stanton to the abolitionists' cause. James Birney and the Grimke sisters, Sarah and Angelina, worked with Weld and his group. Opposition between abolitionist and proslavery forces became increasingly violent until in 1837 an abolitionist editor, Elijah P. Lovejoy, was murdered in Illinois for his abolitionist view. Further fuel was poured on the fire by the publication of *Uncle Tom's Cabin* in 1852 by Harriet Beecher Stowe, the daughter of Lyman Beecher. Methodists and Baptists, particularly in the smaller towns, supported abolition.

Southerners reacted to these aggressive tactics with a vigorous social and religious defense of slavery. Thomas Dew, a professor in William and Mary College, in 1832 published his *Essay on Slavery* as a social rationale of slavery. He argued that an aristocratic group should devote their time to government and culture while slaves did the physical work. This would mean that the Southern aristocratic society like that of classical Athens would rest upon a slave base. Clergymen examined the Old Testament to find religious justification of slavery and found that neither Christ nor Paul had directly attacked slavery in the New Testament. With clergy in the South and the North taking diametrically opposed views, it was little wonder that several denominations finally divided over the slavery issue. The British churches, in contrast, had earlier cooperated to end the slave trade and slavery in England.

Schisms 1843-1861

Because the Baptists emphasized the autonomy of the local congregation and had a minimum of centralization, schism occurred in their missionary organizations. A Baptist foreign missions organization had begun in 1814 to support the work of Judson, who had become a Baptist, and the Baptist Home Missionary Society had been organized in 1832. These societies drew their support from both the South and the North. When the Georgia Baptist Convention of 1844 recommended a slaveholder, James Reeve, for a home missionary and the board turned him down as

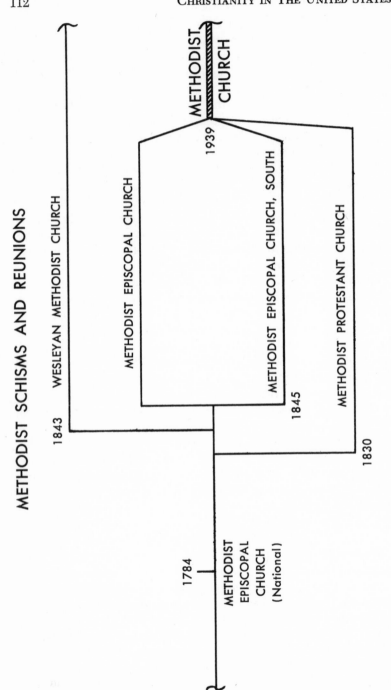

METHODIST SCHISMS AND REUNIONS

WESLEYAN METHODIST CHURCH

METHODIST EPISCOPAL CHURCH

METHODIST EPISCOPAL CHURCH, SOUTH

METHODIST PROTESTANT CHURCH

METHODIST CHURCH

METHODIST EPISCOPAL CHURCH (National)

1784

1830

1843

1845

1939

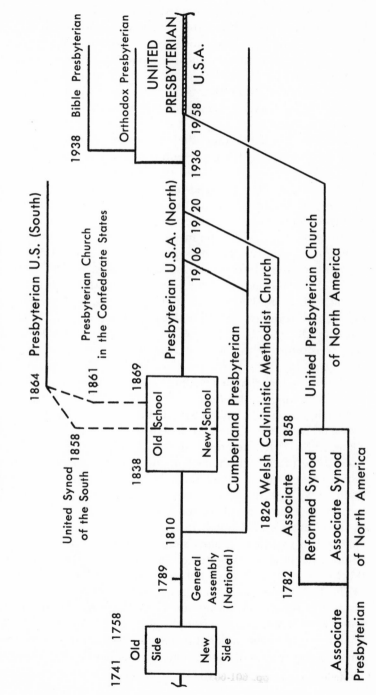

PRESBYTERIAN SCHISMS AND REUNIONS

a slaveholder, the Southern Baptists organized a Southern board for home missions. When the Alabama Baptist Convention in 1844 asked whether slaveholders could become foreign missionaries, the foreign missions board replied that they could not. The Southern churches then organized a Southern Baptist Convention at a meeting in Atlanta, Georgia, in 1845. Thus was born among the Baptists a schism over slavery which has not yet been healed by reunion.

At about the same time the Methodist church divided. As early as 1843 delegates representing about six thousand Methodists met at Utica and formed the Wesleyan Methodist church in opposition to slavery. The major break came, however, over the case of Bishop James O. Andrew of Georgia, who had by marriage come to be an owner of slaves.[4] The request that he resign in the General Conference of 1844 led to a meeting of the Southern Methodists at Louisville, Kentucky, in 1845 and the founding of the Methodist Episcopal Church, South. Not until 1939 did the Methodists of the North and South reunite.

The schism and consequent split among the Presbyterians was much more complex. By 1838 the Presbyterian church had split into the Old and New School groups. The large bloc of antislavery supporters in the New School body in the General Assembly of 1857, aided by many antislavery memorials, secured resolutions which banned support of slavery as a scriptural or divinely ordained institution. In 1858 the Southerners in the New School organized the United Synod of the South with about fifteen thousand members. The Old School in the South did not suffer a split until 1861, when the Old School Southern group withdrew from those of the Old School in the North. The two Southern schisms were united when the Old School Southerners merged their forces with the United Synod of the South in 1864 to form the Presbyterian Church in the Confederate States, now known as the Presbyterian Church in the United States. The Old and New School Northern groups merged in 1869 in the Presbyterian Church in the United States of America. The two branches in the North and South have not yet been reunited.

The Episcopalians took no basic stand on the issue. Although physically separated during the Civil War, the Southern delegates were again seated after the war as if they had not been unable to attend the national meetings. Because the bulk of their membership was antislavery and in the North, the Congregationalists were not troubled by the slavery issue. Neither the Lutherans nor the Roman Catholics took an official stand on the issue. Thus for these churches the only separation was that enforced by the war itself.

These disputes in the churches over slavery have left a bitter heritage in some cases. Neither the Baptists nor Presbyterians, who split before the Civil War, have yet reunited for various reasons. After the war the Negroes increasingly organized their own denominations rather than cooperate with their former white masters in church matters. The spiritual schism preceded the political and geographical schism between North and South.

BIBLIOGRAPHY

BARNES, GILBERT H. *The Anti-Slavery Impulse, 1830-1844.* Gloucester, Mass.: Peter Smith, 1957.

DUMOND, DWIGHT L. *Anti-Slavery Origins of the Civil War in the United States.* Ann Arbor, Mich.: University of Michigan Press, 1939. Able accounts of the religious attack on slavery.

FILLER, LOUIS. *The Crusade against Slavery, 1830-1860.* New York: Harper & Brothers, 1960. An able account of the antislavery movement based on new information.

FOX, EARLY L. *The American Colonization Society, 1817-1840.* Baltimore: Johns Hopkins Press, 1919. An able work on colonization.

OLMSTEAD. *HRUS.* Pp. 362-383.

SWEET. *SRA.* Pp. 285-309.

THOMAS, BENJAMIN P. *Theodore Weld, Crusader for Freedom.* New Brunswick, N.J.: Rutgers University Press, 1950.

17

THE CHURCH IN WAR AND RECONSTRUCTION

THE MORAL ISSUE OF SLAVERY was the first major test that the church faced just before the Civil War in the area of social morality as opposed to individual morality. Both in the North and the South the churches looked upon the war as a crusade for the cause upheld by the respective areas. The division of the country geographically did not come until long after the ecclesiastical divisions of the church over slavery.

The Churches' Attitude to War

The attitude of the Northern churches to the war may be summed up in the expressive thought of Julia Ward Howe's patriotic song that as Christ had died to make men holy so Northern Christians should die to make colored men free. Ministers, serving as individuals, sought to aid the cause. Archbishop John Hughes toured Europe in 1861 to create Roman Catholic goodwill for the Union. Henry Ward Beecher as well as other Protestants also visited England to stir up sentiment favorable to the Union cause. The patriotic fervor of the Northern Old School Presbyterians, expressed in Gardner Spring's resolution of loyalty to the federal government and to the Constitution, brought about the withdrawal of the Old School Presbyterians from the South in 1861. The leaders of the Episcopal church called the roll of Southern dioceses in 1862 as if there had been no break in fellowship even though no Southern delegates were present, but the church did support the Union cause. Lutherans, Methodists, Baptists, Roman Catholics and Jews patriotically supported the war. But the Quakers and other pacifist groups were conscientious objectors whom the government allowed to do humanitarian work.

The churches of the South were equally loyal to the Confederate cause. The seceding Old School Presbyterians formed the Presbyterian Church of the Confederate States in 1861 and in 1864 reunited with the Southern New School United Synod to form what eventually became the Presbyterian Church in the United States. Southern Presbyterians, Roman Catholics, Lutherans, and Baptists were intensely loyal to the Confederate cause.

The Churches' Ministry During the War

Although church leaders did bless the respective cause on both sides and recruited men for the armies by fiery preaching in some cases, the churches quickly assumed responsibility for the moral and spiritual welfare of the soldiers and engaged in humanitarian activities to relieve the physical needs of war sufferers. This was true in both the North and the South.

Southern generals like Jackson and Lee were quite religious and welcomed the provision of chaplains by the churches for their regiments and the visits to the camps by other Southern clergymen. In fact, a great revival broke out in the Confederate armies in 1863 and 1864. It seems to have originated in 1861 in the army camps around Richmond and spread throughout the Southern armies. Estimates of the number of soldier converts run as high as one hundred thousand. Regimental churches were formed with army officers serving as church officers under the chaplains. Both Northern and Southern Bible societies provided Southern soldiers with Bibles, which were passed through the two lines of the opposing armies.

The Northern churches were just as diligent in supplying moral, spiritual and humanitarian aid to their soldiers. Regularly accredited clergymen were by government action accepted as regimental chaplains, and some were also attached to hospitals to serve the wounded and dying. A meeting in New York in 1861 as a result of the endeavors of YMCA leaders brought the United States Christian Commission[1] into being to provide Bibles, religious books, magazines, tracts, and religious services to supplement those of the chaplains. Between 1861 and 1866 this organization spent several million dollars which enabled five thousand unpaid volunteers to give out millions of Bibles, hymnbooks, books, magazines and tracts to the soldiers in the Union army. D. L. Moody, who was to become a great evangelist, was one such very efficient agent during the war. The American Bible Society provided millions of copies of both the Bible and its parts for distribution to Northern soldiers and, with the consent of the

[1]Peter G. Mode, *Sourcebook and Bibliographical Guide to American Church History* (Menasha, Wis.: George Banta Publishing Co., 1921), pp. 618-622.

Northern commanders who let the consignments go through the lines, many also for the Confederate armies. Henry Bellows founded the United States Sanitary Commission in 1861 to provide men who would care for sick and wounded soldiers in the hospitals and help their needy dependents.

Voluntary manumission and the extension of Lincoln's Emancipation Proclamation of 1863 to Southern territory by the freeing of slaves by the advancing Union armies raised the problem of how to care for these colored freedmen. The Union government through the Freedmen's Bureau, organized in March, 1865, under the leadership of General Oliver O. Howard, provided more than fifteen million dollars for the purchase and distribution of fuel, food and clothes for the needy freedmen.

Religious groups had earlier organized Freedmen's Relief Associations to carry on the same kind of work under private auspices. These denominational associations were finally unified into the American Freedmen's Union Commission in 1866 to eliminate duplication of effort. Religious groups also provided educational opportunity for freedmen by setting up schools to give at least elementary education.

Southern churches and their clergymen were not as well treated by the Northern churches as the freedmen were, because of their strong support of the Confederate cause during the war and their justification of slavery before the war. Missionaries were sent from the North to take over and man vacant Southern churches despite the protests of these churches. Lincoln did not approve of Stanton's orders which turned control of Southern Methodist churches over to Northern clergymen, and he countermanded the orders when he became aware of the situation. Dr. Samuel B. McPheeters, minister of a Presbyterian church in St. Louis, was deposed from his pulpit and ordered out of Missouri by a Union general mainly because in 1862 he had christened a child with the name of a Confederate general. Lincoln wrote the Union general to the effect that the army must not interfere with the Southern churches so long as they observed public order and peace. Such interference with the Southern churches did much to create bitter feelings between the sections.

The Churches' Losses in War

Despite the increased giving by the Northern churches during the war, morality and spirituality declined because secular war interests came first. The fratricidal nature of the war seemed to provide more occasion for brutality, especially in the care of prisoners of war on both sides. Much church property was destroyed in the south, in areas such as Atlanta, as the Union armies moved south. The church, both in condemning slavery in the North and supporting it in the South, participated in politics as an organization in a way that compromised its spiritual message. Fortunately evidences of spiritual renewal through the work of the YMCA and other organizations became apparent near the end of the war.

The Churches in Reconstruction

After Lincoln's assassination, his policy of forgiveness to the South gave way to the policy of vengeance of the radicals in Congress in spite of Andrew Johnson's conciliatory spirit. The Emancipation Proclamation of 1863 had set slaves free but had not provided civil liberties. The Thirteenth Amendment, which became law in 1865, gave citizenship and legal rights to the Negro. The churches of the North generally supported this measure as justice to the Negro. Efforts were also made to send missionaries to the South to take over Southern churches, but when the Methodist Episcopal church did take over some churches of its Southern sister church, Johnson returned them to the Southern denomination as soon as he became aware of the situation.

The divided Baptist, Presbyterian and Methodist churches, which had been created by the schisms over slavery, did not reunite during the period of reconstruction, but the Old and New School wings of the Presbyterian church did reunite. The plan for reunion was referred to the presbyteries by the General Assemblies of 1869, and the union of the two bodies became a reality in 1870. Moreover, Southern Episcopalians were also brought back into fraternal fellowship with their Northern brethren at the end of the war.

Much attention was given by the Northern churches during the reconstruction era to the improvement of the lot of the Negro. The various Freedmen's Associations had founded elementary schools in the South for Negroes. As the Southern states assumed responsibility for elementary education for the Negroes, the religious organizations gave more attention to secondary and higher education. The predominantly Congregational American Missionary Association was responsible for the founding of such Negro institutions of higher learning as Fisk University in 1866 and Hampton Institute in 1868 in Virginia.

Only about 12 percent or more than five hundred thousand Negroes who were in the United States in 1860 were members of the churches. Although the Southern denominations tried to make provision for Negroes in their churches, the Negroes because of suspicion of their old masters preferred to set up separate and independent Negro denominations. Methodist Negroes were organized in 1870 into a Methodist Episcopal church with the consent of the white Methodist Episcopal Church, South. Larger numbers turned to the Baptist church because of its democratic, loose polity and its colorful baptism by immersion. Several Baptist Negro denominations came into being. Some Negroes also formed separate Presbyterian and Episcopal denominations, but seemed to prefer the Baptist and Methodist theology and polity.

Unfortunate tendencies soon appeared in some of these Negro denominations. Their emotional outlook often made services more an entertainment than worship of God. Demagogic colored leaders in urban areas on occasion used their members as political tools. Sexual and financial irresponsibility of colored leadership often injured the Negro Christian cause, and their eschatological interest sometimes led them to ignore social problems. But mainly within the framework of Methodist and Baptist theology and church government, the Negro churches with their spirituals have made a cultural contribution to their land as well as meeting their own spiritual needs.

The Churches' Heritage from War

Schism is still one of the heritages of the Civil War. The Baptist and Presbyterian denominations created by schism over slavery before the Civil War still exist. The colored people are also still separated into their own denominations. The political predominance of the Democratic Party in the South has not yet given way to a two-party structure even in the political thinking of many religious leaders of the South. The grave economic, social and political as well as religious problems created by segregation are still part of the bitter fruits of the Civil War. This has left a legacy of hatred between Southern white and Negro as well as hatred in the South for the North because of the often unprincipled activity of the carpetbaggers during the period of reconstruction. The high prewar cultural development of the South was somewhat set back as college buildings were destroyed, students recruited into the army and economic support diverted to the war effort. Present efforts to solve these problems offer much encouragement for the future.

BIBLIOGRAPHY

DUNHAM, CHESTER F. *The Attitude of the Northern Clergy Toward the South, 1860-1865.* Toledo: Gray Publishing Co., 1942. A critical account of the attitude and acts of the Protestant clergy during the war.

OLMSTEAD. *HRUS.* Pp. 384-410.

SWEET. *SRA.* Pp. 312-332.

WEATHERFORD, WILLIS D. *American Churches and the Negro.* Boston: Christopher Publishers, 1957.

WOODSON, CARTER G. *The History of the Negro Church* (2nd ed.). Washington, D.C.: Associated Publishers, 1945. Scholarly studies of the relation of the Negro to the church.

FROM SCHISM AND IDEALISM
TO
ABSOLUTISM AND ECUMENICALISM
(1877 - Present)

18

POST-CIVIL WAR PROBLEMS

ALTHOUGH reconstruction haunted the American public until 1877, other major problems soon became apparent. A moral letdown followed the war; immigration presented the problem of absorbing and Americanizing the millions who poured into the country; the growth of cities offered major problems for solution; and the new western frontier posed problems that seemed almost too great to meet. The church soon recognized these problems and offered what solutions she could to help solve them or at least to cope with the symptoms.

Moral Decline

The crises of war may temporarily turn the minds of people to religion, but as a general rule release from the tensions and danger of war leads to decline in public and private morals. Certainly this was the case in the United States in the period following the Civil War. The idealism of abolitionism and other social reforms gave way to a pragmatism which led to a race for wealth in the expansion of the factory system and the growth of the cities of the land. Moral corruption seemed to affect all classes and areas of society.

Although President Grant seems to have been personally free from corruption, the same was not true of those whom he placed in high positions in the American government. He condemned

James Fisk but used his lavish boats. He also used Cornelius Vanderbilt's private car to travel to the horse races at Saratoga. His followers did not stop with association with these unscrupulous money-makers. Orville E. Babcock, who as secretary controlled Grant's daily list of visitors, became involved in the "Whiskey Ring" in St. Louis, which defrauded the government of millions of dollars. Only Grant's interference saved Babcock from prison. W. W. Belknap, secretary of war during the latter part of Grant's administration, was impeached for accepting large amounts of money from traders in the Indian Territory.

If corruption was the order of the day in national government, scandal and graft were all too prevalent in city government. Although estimates vary, the Tweed ring in control of local government in New York City took between fifty and two hundred million dollars from the city treasury between 1868 and 1871. No attention was paid to the pressing problems of the slums, the new urban immigrants from overseas or the rural areas other than to exploit their votes to control local government.

Moral decline was even more evident in business, which spent much to corrupt legislators at all levels of government. The transfer of the evolutionary dogma of survival of the fittest from biology to society by Herbert Spencer seemed to justify the principle of the survival of the fittest in business. Cornelius Vanderbilt fought Jay Gould and Daniel Drew for control of the Erie Railroad. When Vanderbilt tried to buy enough stock to get control of the railroad, Drew kept on issuing more stock for him to buy. Vanderbilt finally pulled out when the others bought him off by emptying the Erie treasury. Drew also withdrew from the Erie. Under the leadership of John D. Rockefeller, the Standard Oil Company would first undersell all local competition and then when it was eliminated recoup its losses by high charges for a product on which it had a monopoly. Large shipments of oil enabled Rockefeller to get secret rebates from the railways. Businessmen also bought legislators in municipal, state and national government to get franchises, tariff protection for their products and other favors. They paid the acquiescent legislators well for these favors.

Even the church was not immune from scandal. Henry Ward Beecher, the popular preacher of the day who sanctified business success, became involved in charges of adultery with the wife of his associate, Theodore Tilton, the editor of the *Independent*. Tilton sued for alienation of his wife's affections, but Beecher was finally cleared in the trial. The New York superintendent of police reported in 1864 that there were nearly six hundred houses of prostitution in New York City. The church seemed to do little in condemnation of the lowered moral standards in government or business.

The flow of liquor was increased and made respectable as a source of government revenue by the wartime federal tax. In the twenty years between 1860 and 1880 capital in liquor increased more than sixfold from $29,000,000 in 1860. Little wonder that a Prohibition party appeared in 1869 and that the Women's Christian Temperance Union came into being in 1874 to combat the evil of intemperance.

The Problems of Westward Expansion

Much of the area of the Great Plains was still a frontier inhabited by Indians and buffalo at the end of the Civil War. By 1890, when the frontier officially came to an end, great masses of people lured by cheap land had been moved west by the transcontinental railroads. Railroad mileage doubled to seventy thousand miles between 1865 and 1872. The Homestead Act of 1862 offered one hundred sixty acres of land free to those who would settle and improve it for five years. The subjugation of the Indians by the federal government made the area safer for settlement. The agricultural frontier was matched by the wealth to be gained on the cattle frontier of the Southwest. A steer worth five dollars would be worth ten times that amount after four years of free grazing. The mining frontier opened up in Colorado and Nevada drew many. Between 1858 and 1888 more than three hundred and forty million dollars in silver was taken out of the Comstock Lode in Nevada.

Settlers, particularly those on farms on the plains, suffered much. Droughts in summer, blizzards in winter, such as that of 1888, grasshopper plagues, part of the twelve million buffaloes overrunning their crops, and for the women extreme loneliness on the vast expanses of prairie were grave problems. Occasional Indian attacks made life even more perilous.

The church, which also prospered with the rising economy, had resources to meet the needs of the frontier. The value of the resources of the church more than doubled to three hundred fifty-four million dollars between 1860 and 1870. While population rose 65 percent between 1850 and 1870, church membership increased by 84 percent in the same period.

Part of these added assets went into missionary work of the church on the new western frontier to meet the needs of the settlers and the Indians. Methodists, Baptists and Presbyterians organized extension agencies after the Civil War and spent increasing millions to take religion to the frontiersmen. The Baptist Home Missionary Society persuaded the Union Pacific and Central Pacific railroads to grant land for churches and manses in towns on their routes. Chaplain C. C. McCabe proved to be an able leader in the extension of Methodism in the West and twitted Ingersoll in a telegram with the fact that, far from religion dying out, the Methodists were bringing a new church into being each day of the year. Even the Congregationalists in the national Albany Convention in 1852 gave up the Plan of Union and soon raised more than sixty thousand dollars to plant new churches in the West. Other churches soon followed suit.

The Presbyterian Sheldon Jackson (1834-1909) was one of the ablest representatives of his church in the West. After the Civil War he worked as superintendent of Presbyterian missions in the agricultural West. He developed a church building whose sections, fabricated in Chicago, could be shipped anywhere and put up quickly and inexpensively where needed. From 1882 to 1907 his energies were devoted to the problems of what is now the state of Alaska. It was he who in 1892 began to import reindeer from Siberia to provide the Eskimos with food and transportation. He also was put in charge of education in Alaska.

The Indians, who were crowded into reservations after their subjugation by armed force, were not neglected by the church. Schools, hospitals and missions were set up to educate, heal and convert these new wards of society.

The Problems of Immigration

The lure of free land, well advertised abroad by railroads eager to dispose of the land granted to them by the government; the spell of gold and silver on the mining frontier; and the need for labor in the factories of the large corporations of the growing cities brought a large number of immigrants from abroad. Migrants from the rural areas who were no longer needed on the farm because of the increase of efficient labor-saving machinery also came to the cities. Horatio Alger success stories promised wealthy city patrons to virtuous farm boys who could thus soon make their fortune by hard work and virtue.

Corporations, railways and steamship lines all sought to lure people to the New World. From 1861 to 1870 nearly 2,325,000 came to the United States, and in the next decade more than 2,800,000. Between 1881 and 1890 nearly 5,300,000 immigrants arrived. In 1882 alone nearly 640,000 were admitted, of whom more than 250,000 were from Germany, over 100,000 from Great Britain and another 100,000 from the Scandinavian countries. Between 1865 and 1900 around 13,500,000 immigrants entered the United States. Until 1890 most of the immigrants were middle-class, Protestant rural people from northwestern Europe. After that date more came from the agrarian, Roman Catholic areas of central and southeastern Europe. By 1910 foreign immigrants along with Negroes made up two-thirds of the workers in American industry.

These people increased urban problems, since in many cases in the immigration after 1890 they were uneducated and ignorant of urban ways. They became easy prey of demagogues who partially cared for their most pressing needs and collected their votes. Most of these urban immigrants were Roman Catholic and, as a consequence, practiced the "Continental Sabbath," which meant that after attendance at Sunday morning mass the balance of the day could be devoted to recreation.

The Problems of Urbanization

Urban population rose rapidly after the Civil War. Between 1860 and 1890 cities with more than 8,000 people increased in number from 141 to 547. City dwellers numbered about one-fifth of the population in 1860, but by 1900 constituted more than two-fifths of the population of nearly 76,000,000. Between 1860 and 1900 the population of New York increased more than 300 per cent. By the end of the century Chicago was second only to New York in population.

These new cities grew up without planning. Unscrupulous promoters exploited the new population by crowding homes along gridiron streets without saving any desirable sections for parks. Slums multiplied as a result. Stream pollution by factory and sewage waste increased. Crooked politicians exploited the new ignorant voters to gain control of city and state treasuries, which they then looted for their own gain.

When one considers the increase of wealth in town and country in this era along with the very low standards of living, coupled with exploitation of the city masses by the unscrupulous, it is little wonder that historians have referred to the greater part of the period between the Civil War and 1900 as the Gilded Age. How the church reacted to some of the problems discussed above is the burden of the next five chapters.

BIBLIOGRAPHY

Olmstead. *HRUS.* Pp. 410-418.
Sweet. *SRA.* Pp. 332-335, 336-339, 360-362.

Bibliography for Era from 1877 to Present

Atkins, Gaius G. *Religion in Our Times.* New York: Round Table Press, 1932. A perceptive interpretation of the main trends on the American religious scene between 1892 and 1932.

Garrison, Winfred E. *The March of Faith.* New York: Harper & Brothers, 1933. An interesting, readable and objective account of religion in the United States since 1865.

Weisenburger, Francis P. *Ordeal of Faith.* New York: Philosophical Library, 1959. Able presentation of the erosion of faith and the rise of Liberalism from 1865 to 1900.

19

THE CHURCHES AND POST-CIVIL WAR IMMIGRATION

IMMIGRATION brought rapid increases in population in the United States after the Civil War. Until 1890 most of the immigrants were Protestants from northwestern Europe, increasing the numbers of Lutherans markedly. After that date large numbers of Roman Catholics and Jews came to the United States from southeastern Europe to escape, in the case of the Jews, persecution and, in the case of the others, overpopulation and economic or political problems. People of the earlier migrations had tended to settle on farms in the northern part of the Mississippi Valley, but the later migrants moved to cities as factory workers and became difficult to assimilate into American culture. The demand for cheap labor to build the western railroads also brought more than one hundred thousand Chinese into the United States by 1880.

The Roman Catholic Church and Immigrants

By 1865 about two million Irish, who were Roman Catholics, had come to America after the potato famine of 1845. After the failure of the German democratic revolution in 1848, many Roman Catholic Germans arrived. By 1890 large numbers of Roman Catholic peasants were also entering from central and southeastern Europe from countries such as Italy, after the advent of direct steamship service from Mediterranean ports to the United States. French Roman Catholics from Canada came into the northeastern states and Mexican Roman Catholics from the southwest. At the end of the Civil War there were about three million Roman Catholics in the United States or nearly 10 percent of the population, but by 1900 there were four times as many. This constituted a problem of assimilation for that church. Little wonder that after 1908 the United States was freed by the Papacy from the status of being missionary territory.

The church met the challenge by the provision of forty new dioceses between 1881 and 1911 and the development of male and female religious orders in large numbers. By 1930 there were 215 orders of women alone, serving the church in educational and healing ministries. Many of these nuns and monks as well as priests came from Ireland, Germany and France. The need for priests was greatest in the factory and mining cities of the East, where numerous Catholic immigrants settled. But many priests went to the frontier to meet the needs of the expanding Roman Catholic population as well as those of the Indians.

Pius IX expressed opposition to liberal ideas in any area of life in the Syllabus in 1864. The declaration of papal infallibility in 1870 clashed with tendencies to ecclesiastical nationalism in American Catholicism. Isaac Hecker (1819-1888), the founder of the Paulist order to convert Protestants, wanted the American clergy and laity to have freedom for individual initiative in building the church. James Gibbons (1834-1921), a cardinal and archbishop of Baltimore, who opposed the Knights of Columbus organization in 1882, was another who wanted to assimilate American Roman Catholicism into its cultural and democratic environment. Leo XII in 1899 condemned these tendencies to Americanism.

While leaders of the Roman Catholic church were trying to integrate the church into its environment, Protestant forces, fearful lest the large Roman Catholic immigration might make the United States a Roman Catholic country, founded the American Protective Association in 1887. This largely rural movement opposed urban Roman Catholicism and wanted to curb immigration and to prevent public funds from going to parochial schools. The scarcity of jobs in the depression of 1893 accentuated the movement, but by the end of the century it lost its influence and soon disappeared.

The attempt to get public funds for parochial schools by federal or state legislation engendered Protestant opposition. Conservative Roman Catholics opposed efforts to integrate Roman Catholics into the public school system with provision for religious training by the church after school hours. The church finally turned to the parochial system, in which schools were set up in each parish under church control, staffed by the church and paid for by the faithful. The question of the relation of the parochial school to the state has been a perennial source of difficulty between Protestants and Roman Catholics.

Lutheranism and the Immigrants

German and Scandinavian immigrants increased from about five hundred thousand in 1870 to four and a half times that number by 1910. In this period 1,750,000 Scandinavians migrated mainly to Minnesota to become farmers. Not all remained Lutherans because those churches were divided over whether to follow the American Lutheran tendencies of Schmucker (see Chap. 13) and were also plagued with schisms, such as that which created the Augustana Synod in 1860 and those brought about by Civil War divisions. In addition, Lutheran churches tended to form along national or linguistic lines. In 1870 the Norwegians and Danes broke with the Augustana Synod to form churches along linguistic lines. Of all the Lutheran bodies, perhaps the aggressive Missouri Synod profited most by the new immigration and won large numbers into its fold.

Some of the Germans not won by the Lutherans were won by the Baptists, who developed a German department in Rochester Theological Seminary under the leadership of the father of Walter Rauschenbusch. Large numbers of Scandinavians also became Baptists. The Methodist and Reformed churches, the latter because of Dutch immigration, gained in membership. Enough Welsh immigrants became Calvinists to form the Welsh Presbyterian church with its own General Assembly in 1869.

American Judaism and Jewish Immigrants

Sephardic Jews from Spain and Portugal formed the seventeenth century vanguard of Jewish immigration to this country. The failure of the revolution of 1848 in Germany caused many German Jews to come to the United States, where they set up their own synagogues. Later pogroms in eastern Europe caused numbers to flee from there to find freedom from persecution in America.

The very conservative Orthodox Jews upheld both the ethical and ceremonial law as a revelation of God's will which must be kept by Jews. They also observed strict dietary laws and the keeping of the Sabbath, and used only Hebrew in their services. They looked for a Messiah and His kingdom as the culmination of world history. Others, such as the Reform and Conservative groups, were more willing to adapt to their new environment. The B'nai B'rith order, founded in 1843, was an attempt to unite American Jewry along cultural, charitable and even social lines, but it could not overcome the fissiparous tendencies created by immigration.

Liberal Reform Judaism developed, mainly under the leadership of Isaac M. Wise (1819-1900). By 1873 he had brought about the creation of a council of Reform congregations. In 1875 the council opened the Hebrew Union College in Cincinnati to train rabbis for Reform Judaism. The Reform Jews gave up the dietary aspects of the law, the hope of the coming of a personal Messiah and the restoration of Jews in Palestine. Like Protestant liberals, they adopted the ideas of progressive revelation and anti-supernaturalism. They gave up national identity, but retained the idea of a religious community which would spread Jewish religious and moral ideals among all men to achieve a Messianic age.

The Conservative synagogues linked up with the groups from eastern Europe to found the Jewish Theological Seminary in New York in 1885. Solomon Schecter became the president. These groups kept the Jewish law and the Hebrew language, but weakened the prophetic element of the Old Testament in the attempt to integrate their ancient faith and modern culture. The Conservatives rank after the Orthodox and Reform groups in size. Most Jews tend to stress ethics above theology, deed above creed.

Anti-Semitism has been a perennial problem for modern Jewry. Pogroms in eastern Europe forced many to migrate. By 1914 there were three million Jews in the United States. This persecution led to the organization of the Zionist movement by Theodore Herzl (1860-1904) at a meeting in Basel in 1879. Reform congregations opposed it, but those who had been or were being persecuted favored it. The Balfour Declaration of the British government in 1917, promising a national home in Palestine for the Jews, stimulated the movement. Desire to migrate to the homeland became stronger during World War II, when Hitler in 1939 exterminated about six million of the sixteen million Jews in the world. Israel became an independent state in 1948.

The Orthodox Churches in the United States

The Russian Orthodox church was planted in Alaska when it was a Russian possession. After Alaska was purchased by the United States in 1867, the church expanded southward along the coast until the bishop was able to move to San Francisco in 1872. Immigration from eastern Europe created so many new churches in the eastern United States that in 1905 the episcopal center was moved to New York. After the revolution of 1917 in Russia, the Russian Orthodox church became an independent body in the *Sobor* of 1924. Most of its members were laborers.

The Greek Orthodox church found its following among the small businessmen with restaurants, flower shops and confectionery stores. These people had migrated from Greece in large numbers. It too became an independent church, free from control of the Old Land, in the twentieth century. Other national groups also founded Orthodox churches in this country, but they were much smaller than the above two. All these groups permitted much more lay participation in the affairs of the church than did the parent bodies in Europe.

This chapter reveals that the Lutherans and the Roman Catholics profited most from immigration after the Civil War. The problems of relations between the Papacy and American Catholics and the persistence of national Lutheran churches were the most pronounced difficulties. Independence from European leadership was the major problem of the Orthodox churches, while the question of assimilation of the culture of the adopted land vexed the Jews.

BIBLIOGRAPHY

EMHARDT, WILLIAM C., *et al. The Eastern Church in the Western World.* Milwaukee: Morehouse Publishing Co., 1928.

GLAZER, NATHAN. *American Judaism.* Chicago: University of Chicago Press, 1957. An able history of Judaism in the United States.

OLMSTEAD. *HRUS.* Pp. 419-445.

SWEET. *SRA.* Pp. 340, 341, 362-371, 379-385.

20

MEETING THE URBAN CHALLENGE

THE RAPID RISE in urban population after the Civil War has already been noted (see Chap. 18). This increase created many new problems for the churches. Country churches were weakened as young people were attracted to the cities to make a living in the factories because mechanization on the farm lessened the area of employment. The "Continental Sunday" with the afternoon devoted to pleasure after attendance at the mass in the morning, coupled with an increased urban commercialization and debasement of pleasure, tended to secularize Sunday. Sweatshops, dirty tenements (sometimes owned by churches), garbage-strewn streets with little room for traffic, and corrupt governments characterized such cities as New York in this period. Settlement of the immigrants in the downtown areas caused the native-born to flee to the suburbs. This confronted the church with the dilemma of whether to serve the inner city or to follow middle-class parishioners to the suburbs. Protestantism also faced the challenge of its relationship to an expanding Roman Catholic population which seemed to threaten its dominant position in American society.

The churches did their best to meet the challenge of the city by the development of various new techniques and ministries. The basic activism of the American churches was well demonstrated in this era. Unfortunately, too often the ministries dealt with the symptoms of evils rather than attacking their basic causes. Downtown missions met many of the needs of the down-and-out but did little about the causes for the emergence of such individuals. Often a too optimistic outlook led to the conviction that the kingdom of God could be achieved by human effort.

The concentration of population in urban areas coupled with the building of large churches made possible the rise of *princes of the pulpit* who tried to arouse people to the existence of social problems and to seek social as well as personal answers to these problems. Phillips Brooks (1835-1893) defined preaching as "the impartation of truth through personality" in his 1877 Yale Lectures on Preaching. After ministering in Philadelphia for ten years, he was called to Trinity Church in Boston. He became the favorite preacher of that city with his ability to put spiritual ideas into words that arrested the hearer and demanded action. From him came the lovely Christmas hymn "O Little Town of Bethlehem." Henry Ward Beecher (1813-1887), pastor of Plymouth Church in Brooklyn from 1847 until his death, was an eloquent, dramatic and witty preacher who opposed injustices, such as slavery, from his pulpit. He was also an able editor and writer of leading Christian papers of the day. His successor, Lyman Abbott (1835-1922), devoted his more conversational type of preaching to popularizing evolution and attempting to integrate it into Christian theology. Thomas deWitt Talmage (1832-1902) had a more florid delivery for his sensational sermons with their sentimental approach to personal salvation. These men and many others had wide influence upon the population of great cities.

Urban organized mass evangelism by professional evangelists, apart from the work of Finney and his successors in the eastern part of the United States, was developed after the Civil War to meet the challenge of winning the urban masses to the church. Previous revivals also had been more spontaneous.

Dwight L. Moody (1837-1899) was a pioneer in this field. A shoe salesman in a Boston store, he was converted through the efforts of his Sunday school teacher, Edward Kimball. In 1856 Moody moved to Chicago and soon prospered in the same business. At first he brought street urchins to Sunday school, but soon opened his own mission Sunday school. During the Civil War he served with the United States Christian Commission. For some years after the war he spent time promoting the work of the YMCA and collected money to build a large one in Chicago. Following this he went to England with Ira D. Sankey, a layman with great musical ability. The two men published the well-known *Sacred Songs and Solos.* More than one million dollars in royalties from sales of ten million copies of this hymnbook was devoted to the support of Moody's schools at Northfield. The British campaign between 1873 and 1875 launched this never-ordained layman into large-scale campaigns in Brooklyn, Philadelphia, New York, Chicago, Boston, Baltimore and St. Louis. These meetings were conducted only at the invitation of all the evangelical ministers of a city and were highly organized, with publicity and counselors for the inquirers. Moody's simple theology of salvation from sin by faith in Christ, the Son of the loving God, was directed both to the emotions and reason. Moody Memorial Church in Chicago carries on the tradition of his ministry. Moody also sponsored educational work. Northfield Seminary for girls and Mount Hermon School for boys were founded by him. Later, in 1886, Moody Bible Institute grew out of his desire to give Bible training to lay workers. He was also largely responsible for the Student Volunteer Movement for Foreign Missions. It had its beginnings in a meeting at Northfield in 1886 which inspired one hundred students to such service.

Several evangelists followed Moody's pattern of evangelism. R. A. Torrey, J. Wilbur Chapman, "Gipsy" (Rodney) Smith and particularly Billy Sunday held mass evangelistic meetings in large cities. William A. Sunday (1863-1935), a former professional baseball player, was converted in Pacific Garden Mission and, from 1895 on, became known (with Homer A. Rodeheaver becoming his song leader after 1900) as an evangelist who used sensational methods to win people. He, like others of the mass evangelists, attacked social evils, such as booze. Thus the era between Reconstruction and World War I was dominated in the field of evangelism by these remarkable men who won thousands for the church.

With the increase in church membership from 16 percent of the population in 1850 to 36 percent in 1900 and an increase in national wealth, it was natural for the church to give more attention to the *layman* as a source of service to the cause of Christ. Men with wealth from industry gave generously and in return were rewarded by positions of influence in the churches. Business efficiency and methods were used in financing church work. Laymen were given representation on church boards, committees and conferences. Men like Jay Cooke, John D. Rockefeller, Daniel Drew, Cyrus H. McCormick and others were loyal churchmen and church workers in spite of their sometimes questionable business tactics. They not only gave money to churches but provided finance for the foundation of seminaries and colleges, such as McCormick Seminary in Chicago, Drew Seminary and the University of Chicago. Groups for men were founded in the churches. The American Christian Commission recommended the use of women missionaries for work in the cities, and several denominations created training institutions to train deaconesses for lay work in hospitals, social services and churches. These were the humble beginnings of the present prominence of the laity in the affairs of the church in this land.

The development of more adequate *religious educational techniques and content* was not neglected as another approach to reaching the urban masses. The American Sunday-School Union from the time of its founding in 1824 had promoted interdenominational Sunday school conventions to provide cooperation of the churches in this important work. The fifth Sunday School Convention at Indianapolis in 1872, at the urging of Bishop John H. Vincent and B. F. Jacobs, a Chicago Baptist layman, adopted the plan of uniform Sunday school lessons. Thus all pupils would be studying the same lessons each Sunday in an attempt to get an integrated view of the whole Bible over a period of years. After 1908 the principle of grading the lessons to fit the age of the pupils was adopted. Organized adult Bible classes began in Marshall A. Hudson's First Baptist Church in Syracuse in 1890, with the Baraca class for young men, and the Philathea class for women in 1895. Daily vacation Bible schools, meeting in the summer vacation period to supplement the work of the Sunday school, had their beginning in the experiment by Robert Boville in his Baptist City Mission in New York in 1901. Released time from the public school schedule to give children religious training in their own churches or, until the McCollum Case in 1947, in school property had its beginning in the work of W. A. Avam, pastor of the First Methodist Church in Gary, Indiana.

The work of coordination of all these efforts at religious education was centered in the Religious Education Association founded in 1903. This was eventually replaced in 1922 by the more liberally oriented International Council of Religious Education, which seemed for a time to be more interested in methods than in the content of teaching. Bishop Vincent had developed teachers' institutes for the better training of Sunday school teachers as early as 1865. In 1874 he and Lewis Miller organized a camp at Chautauqua, New York, where Sunday school teachers could gather for two weeks' training each summer in lovely surroundings. This institution attracted traveling lecturers, such as Russell Conwell, whose lecture "Acres of Diamonds," given by him about six thousand times, brought in eight million dollars, most of which was used to found Temple University. The Chautauqua movement developed into a broad adult educational movement, and chautauquas and chautauqua lecturers appeared all over the country. These various activities and organizations indicate something

of the dynamic nature of the Sunday school movement as one possible answer to reaching the urban masses with Christianity.

The Christian Endeavor Society came into being to help close
the gap between children in the Sunday school and young adults
in the church by providing religious meetings and training in
Christian leadership for youths. The first Christian Endeavor Society was organized in a Congregational church in Portland,
Maine, in 1881 by Francis E. Clark. Young people directed the
society, which provided worship, instruction and social recreation.
The movement grew until in 1892 it had about 1,200,000 members.
Seeing the value of such an approach, a number of denominations
founded young people's organizations, such as the Methodist Epworth League in 1889, the Baptist Young People's Union in 1891,
and the Luther League in 1895. This has led to the eclipse of the
Christian Endeavor movement.

The YMCA had been organized in England in 1844 by George
Williams and several of his friends to provide a home away from
home for young men in the city, where they could have whole-
some surroundings, social life apart from the evils of commer-
cialized amusement, and educational and religious activities that
would promote intellectual and spiritual growth. The first American Y was opened in Boston in 1851, and by 1861 there were over
two hundred such organizations throughout the country. The
YMCA promoted the revival of 1857 and 1858 and was responsible
for the creation of the Christian Commission during the Civil
War. The YWCA was brought to the United States first in 1866 in
Boston to meet similar needs of young women.

Many organizations to provide *social service under Christian
auspices* in the urban environment came into being also between
1865 and 1914. Nondenominational city missions, to meet the
physical and spiritual needs of the people of skid rows in various
cities, had their origin with the founding of the mission on New
York's Water Street in 1872 by Jerry McAuley, a former drunkard
and burglar. Pacific Garden Mission in Chicago, founded in 1877
by Colonel and Mrs. George R. Clarke, is another notable illustration of this type of institution. William Booth's Salvation Army
was organized in England in 1878 to reach the poor of the cities
and came to the United States in 1880 with the arrival of George
S. Railton and seven women. Ballington Booth, son of the founder, took charge of the American Salvation Army in 1886, and it
grew rapidly. Salvation preaching on the street with vocal and
instrumental music was supplemented by social service through

homes for children and delinquent girls, employment agencies and farm colonies to help former drunkards get on their feet. In 1896 Ballington Booth broke with the hierarchical military organization and founded the more democratic Volunteers of America.

An even larger movement was that of the *institutional church*. The church was designed to reach the family on Sunday and prayer meeting night, but the institutional church sought to minister to the whole person seven days a week. It was an attempt to meet the needs of the inner city where congregations were fleeing to the suburbs leaving the needy inner city unchurched. The institutional church provided religious training and social and recreational activities in gymnasiums and handicraft facilities, classes for expectant mothers, and libraries. Thus the church adapted to its environment rather than fleeing from it. The origin of the name has been credited to William J. Tucker, a former president of Dartmouth. William A. Muhlenberg, grandson of the colonial Muhlenberg, pioneered the introduction of social services in his New York Episcopal parish as early as 1846. Thomas K. Beecher seems to have been the first consciously to organize his church, the First Congregational Church of Elmira, New York, along institutional lines, with the provision of a gymnasium, classrooms, a library and other equipment for a social program. St. George's Episcopal Church on New York's East Side under the leadership of the new rector W. S. Rainsford and with the generous financial support of J. P. Morgan, one of his vestrymen, became in 1882 an institutional church at a cost of more than two million dollars between 1883 and 1899. Russell Conwell's Baptist Temple of Philadelphia was organized along institutional lines by 1891, and Temple University grew out of the church's night school for working people. Many other churches also followed the institutional pattern. Most eventually became social settlements.

The Goodwill Industries was founded in 1902 in the Methodist church of Edgar J. Helms in Boston. Handicapped workers were employed in renovating old clothes, furniture and appliances for sale to poor people at low prices. The money was used to pay the handicapped. By 1953 it had more than one hundred factories with three hundred fifty stores and sales worth fourteen million dollars.

Cooperative social action to analyze the problems of the cities and to seek solutions to them became the duty of the American Christian Commission, founded in 1865 as the result of the work of James E. Yeatman. A monthly newspaper, *The Christian at*

Work, promoted the program of visitation of the poor, rescue of social misfits, the use of women missionaries, and united Christian action to detect and to solve urban problems.

The large investment in the liquor industry after the Civil War brought with it the problem of drunkenness, and Christian groups began to agitate for *temperance* and even *prohibition.* By 1898 many towns and five states had voted in prohibition by local option. The Women's Christian Temperance Union, which came into being in 1874, campaigned for temperance with great vigor after Frances Willard became its president in 1879. The churches, particularly the Methodist and Baptist, cooperated with the Anti-Saloon League of America after its founding in 1895. The work of these organizations was crowned by the adoption of the Eighteenth Amendment in 1919. The Volstead Act of 1920 defined illegal beverages in order to put the amendment into effect.

With the increased number of immigrants, the churches fought the relaxation of the Puritan Sunday by the creation of organizations to bring about the enforcement of Sunday closing of business. These groups persuaded the authorities of the 1893 World's Fair in Chicago to shut down the machinery on Sunday although the grounds might be opened as a recreational park.

The increase of wealth in the period after 1865 had an impact upon the church which was both beneficial and harmful. The unscrupulous Jay Cooke, who tithed, belonged to the Episcopal church. John D. Rockefeller was a Baptist Sunday school teacher. Cyrus H. McCormick and Daniel Drew gave much wealth to the seminaries which still bear their names. Other prosperous but not so wealthy middle-class businessmen were also interested in the church.

The efficient methods of business were brought over into church management and organization, and businessmen were added to church and church college boards. This tendency led to centralization of the activities of the churches in boards or committees. Such centralization was particularly noticeable in the Presbyterian and Baptist denominations.

Large gifts by businessmen made possible more magnificent church buildings in Gothic and Romanesque styles. Stained-glass windows, cushioned pews and works of art became familiar in many churches. Increasingly formal architecture also had an impact upon the conduct of worship. Pipe organs, gowned and professional choirs, robed ministers and more elaborate ritual and liturgical practices were used even in those churches, such as the

Methodist and Presbyterian, which had been so strong on the frontier.

These changes and practices made the churches become increasingly middle class in their clientele; and the person who did not feel at ease socially or economically in them was lost to the church. In some cases the labor union or lodge headquarters replaced the church. Some people began to attend store-front churches. This helped to strengthen the Holiness groups who made an appeal to the worker by making him feel at home in the service and by presenting the gospel in his language. The larger churches were looked upon as being more liberal. The Social Gospel of Walter Rauschenbusch was a later attempt to correct this situation by relating the life of the church in a corrective fashion to the social problems of the day (see Chap. 23).

Thus the churches sought to meet the many challenges the new urban environment brought to them. These challenges were more difficult in many ways than those presented by the frontier.

BIBLIOGRAPHY

OLMSTEAD. *HRUS*. Pp. 446-465, 475-480, 484-489.
SWEET. *SRA*. Pp. 311, 335, 336, 345-353, 372-375, 385-388.

Religion in the Cities:

ABELL, AARON I. *The Urban Impact on American Protestantism, 1865-1900.* Cambridge: Harvard University Press, 1943. An excellent account of the response of the church to urban problems.

HOPKINS, CHARLES H. *History of the Young Men's Christian Association in America.* New York: Association Press, 1951.

Mass Evangelism:

BRADFORD, GAMALIEL. *D. L. Moody, a Worker in Souls.* New York: George A. Doran Co., 1927. A useful biography.

CURTIS, RICHARD K. *They Called Him Mister Moody.* Garden City, N.Y.: Doubleday & Co., 1962. An objective account of the evangelist's work based on a careful study of the sources.

HARKNESS, ROBERT. *Reuben Archer Torrey, The Man, His Message.* Chicago: Moody Press, 1929. Gives the flavor of Torrey's personality and life.

McLOUGHLIN, WILLIAM G. *Billy Sunday Was His Real Name.* Chicago: University of Chicago Press, 1955. An unsympathetic but full account.

MOODY, WILLIAM R. *The Life of D. L. Moody.* New York: Fleming H. Revell Co., 1900. A scholarly documented biography.

OTTMAN, FORD C. *J. Wilbur Chapman, a Biography.* New York: Doubleday, Page & Co., 1920. A standard biography.

21

URBAN CULTS AND NEW DENOMINATIONS

ADVENTISM, Mormonism and Spiritualism, which had come into being before 1861, moved with much success into the urban industrial environment of America. The problem of polygamy brought the Mormons into conflict with the federal government because the decision to make that practice illegal in 1862 was upheld by the Supreme Court in 1878. Not until 1890 did the Mormon leadership ban plural marriages, and the state constitution prohibited it when Utah was admitted to the Union. Spiritualism became a national movement in 1893 when it created a national organization. In the period after World War I, the desire to communicate with those who died in war and to seek the meaning of death led to a 75 percent increase in its numbers.

Several reasons might help to account for the growth of these three bodies and the emergence of new cults in the city in both the nineteenth and twentieth centuries. Many wealthy women with increased leisure sought to overcome boredom by dabbling in cults. The isolation and loneliness of city life for those who could not adjust easily caused them to seek companionship and a sense of belonging in the cult groups. Churches which moved with their prosperous middle-class members to the suburbs left the downtown areas to be exploited by these more aggressive groups. With liberalism came a lessening of the authority of the Bible, and people turned for certainty to these groups that were authoritarian and seemed to offer positive answers to life's problems. Cults offered easy answers to sin and guilt and disease. In the period of depression after 1929, they helped to solve the problem of economic security by the appeal to positive thinking in Unity, and by cooperative action in the case of Father Divine's cult. Because voluntarism was the keynote of American religious life, it was easy for these new groups to appeal to the spiritually footloose.

141

Philosophical or Metaphysical Cults
Originating Since 1865

Several cults starting after the Civil War seem to have been influenced by the teaching of Phineas P. Quimby (1802-1866), the self-taught son of a blacksmith. He became interested in hypnotism as a mental healing process, which he thought was that which Christ had used. Mrs. Mary Baker Eddy found healing as his patient and became enamored of his theories. Warren F. Evans also practiced Quimby's technique, and New Thought grew out of his work. Through Christian Science, Charles and Myrtle Fillmore were healed and were influenced by Quimby's ideas. They parted from Christian Science and founded the Unity School of Christianity. One should not ignore the possible influence of New England transcendentalism with its emphasis upon the permeation by the divine mind of all that is in the world.

Mrs. Mary Baker Glover Patterson Eddy (1821-1910), who had three husbands, was a weak and somewhat neurotic young woman. Her first marriage to Glover was dissolved by death within six months. In 1853 she married an itinerant dentist, Daniel Patterson, from whom she obtained a divorce in 1873. Later she was married to Asa G. Eddy. She met Quimby in 1862 and was healed of spinal infection by him. Though she denied any influence from Quimby, this experience led her to formulate her ideas in the book *Science and Health,* published in 1875. In the same year the first society was organized in Lynn, Massachusetts, where she was training students in her new "science." A charter was obtained in 1879 for the Church of Christ (Scientist). She moved to Boston in 1882, where the Mother Church of Christian Science came into being in 1892. All Christian Scientists are formed into more than three thousand branch churches of the Mother Church and are under the supervision of its board of directors, a self-perpetuating body. No statistics as to membership are made known. The denomination publishes the *Christian Science Monitor.*

Mrs. Eddy pushed idealistic philosophy to the point where she denied the reality of matter and declared that it was an illusion and an error of mortal mind. God, a spiritual being, alone was real, good and love, and Christ's function was to demonstrate to men the way to become united with God. Because sin, sickness and death were illusions, one would sin by accepting their reality. Healing would come by recognizing their nonexistence.[1] Chris-

[1]Peter G. Mode, *Sourcebook and Bibliographical Guide to American Church History* (Menasha, Wis.: George Banta Publishing Co., 1921), pp. 653-655.

tian Science is gnostic in that only the knowing ones share its benefits. A surprising number of middle-class and intellectual people have been won to this group.

Quimby's principles were also used by Warren F. Evans after Quimby's death in 1866, and in 1914 Evans' New Thought cult became a national organization. This cult exalted the infinity of God, the divinity of man to the point of pantheism and his possibilities for development by thought and obedience to the divine presence within.

Still more popular was Unity, which was organized by Charles and Myrtle Fillmore who had been healed through Christian Science. After breaking with Mrs. Eddy and after a short period in the New Thought group, they founded their Unity movement with its headquarters at Unity City near Kansas City, Missouri. Unity stressed the power of positive thinking to attain success and Christ-consciousness. Psychiana was founded in 1929 by Frank B. Robinson in Idaho as a cult with similar teachings.

Theosophy was another occult and metaphysical cult imported into the United States in 1875 by Helena P. Blavatsky, and the Theosophical Society was founded later with the aid of Henry S. Olcott. It became an independent American society in 1895. Its main branch has its headquarters in Wheaton, Illinois. Leadership of the British wing was taken over by Annie Besant, who had moved from atheism through Spiritualism to Theosophy. The cult reflects Buddhist and Hindu influences. Souls are supposedly transmigrated in successive incarnations to other human bodies and accumulate wisdom concerning God, the source of all. Mahatmas are incarnated to give special wisdom from deity. Mrs. Besant paraded Krishnamurti as one of these mahatmas or messiahs. It will be noticed that in this cult also God and the universe are identified in pantheistic fashion. The aim of the society was to develop universal brotherhood, the study of ancient scriptures and the investigation of the secrets of nature.

The Baha'i cult is an adaptation of a Persian movement founded about the middle of the last century. The Bab, who founded it, claimed to be one of several saviours to teach truth and righteousness. His successors taught the idea of universal peace, the oneness of man and a brotherhood of all faiths. It was imported to this land shortly after World War I. A lovely temple in Wilmette, Illinois, is the American headquarters of this cult. This and the cults previously discussed emphasize the identification of man, God and nature.

Communal Cults

Other cults, particularly during the depression of the thirties, were organized along communistic or communal lines. John A. Dowie (1847-1907) was a Scottish Congregational minister in Australia who built a large tabernacle in Melbourne in 1882. He opposed the use of liquor, drugs and tobacco, and emphasized divine healing and Christ's second coming. In 1890 he came to Chicago after two years in San Francisco. He made the claim that he was Elijah III. He was able to found the Christian Catholic Apostolic Church in 1896. Zion City near Waukegan, Illinois, was set up along communal lines in 1901. Dowie lost control in 1906 and was replaced by Wilbur Glenn Voliva, who argued that the earth was flat. Gradually Zion lost its religious exclusivism, although the church still flourishes there.

Benjamin Purnell founded the House of David in 1903 in Benton Harbor, Michigan. Here he gathered people together to prepare for the imminent end of the world. All their property was put in his name. Scandals over sex and suits for economic malpractice brought against him by his followers caused the communal organization to end.

The Peace Mission of Father Divine, first organized along communal lines in Brooklyn in 1915, attracted many Negroes in the hard times of the thirties. This Negro was accepted as God by his followers. They turned all their earnings over to him, and lived and ate in the various "heavens" which he organized in major cities. Husbands and wives were separated in different quarters to foster celibacy.

Eschatological Cults

Charles T. Russell, who was tortured by fear of hell, after a period of infidelity studied the Bible until he became convinced that hell was not taught in the Bible and that Christ's invisible second coming had already taken place. He looked for a "second chance" for salvation in another life. Christ's essential deity and the validity of the atonement were denied by the idea that Christ is a created being. Russell's followers have been critical of the churches and have clashed with the government over their refusal to salute the flag and their effort to have all their male members considered ministers by Selective Service.

After founding the group in 1872 Russell made Brooklyn his headquarters in 1909. J. F. Rutherford became his successor in

1917. Members of the movement give much time to the distribution of their literature, and the group has an enormous publishing program. They have been known as Jehovah's Witnesses since 1931.

Many of these cults, such as Unity, catered to the desire for material success. Others catered to the need for healing, release from sin and the desire to contact deceased loved ones. Most of these cults found the urban environment a fruitful source of converts and gained consequent wealth and prestige which some of the opportunistic leaders sought. Many of them represent the unpaid bills of churches which neglected some of the teachings that should have been a part of their message.

Evangelistic Organizations

The Foursquare church of Aimee Semple McPherson (1890-1944) is an illustration of a militantly evangelistic group. Mrs. McPherson, who had been a missionary in China, where she lost her first husband, Robert Semple, engaged in evangelism and moved to California in 1918. She soon gathered a faithful following by sensational evangelism and in 1922 built Angelus Temple to seat 5,300 people at a cost of over one million dollars. Her "foursquare" gospel emphasized salvation, healing, speaking in tongues and the second coming of Christ. The work still continues under the leadership of her son Rolf, although her disappearance in 1927 and her two broken marriages cast a cloud on her work.

The Assemblies of God, with similar beliefs, organized in 1914 and now have a claimed membership of more than five hundred thousand. These Pentecostal churches with the Holiness groups, such as the Church of God (Anderson, Ind.), the Free Methodist church founded in 1860, the Church of the Nazarene founded in 1895, and with the Christian and Missionary Alliance organized in 1887, have been termed a "third force." They have practiced a vigorous evangelism and experienced rapid growth.

The Oxford Group grew out of the work of Frank N. D. Buchman(1878-1961), a Lutheran minister who had a special spiritual experience in 1908. He began to travel around the world preaching his gospel of the four absolutes—honesty, purity, love and self-sacrifice—as the fruit of a changed life. Much emphasis was laid upon "sharing" of past sin and religious experiences to help one another and to convert others present at the large house or hotel parties in which the group specialized after 1918. Guidance for the day was to come in a quiet time, and such guidance was to be written down. The appeal was to the spiritually "up-and-out." The group, known outside England by the name of "Moral Rearmament," sought to prevent World War II by "changing" world leaders. The movement minimized the objective authority of the Bible, and the emphasis upon sharing often led to sordid revelations of past sins in the area of sexual irregularity. It did not create a separate church but operated within the regular churches.

BIBLIOGRAPHY

BEASLEY, NORMAN. *The Cross and the Crown*. New York: Duell, Sloan, and Pearce, 1952. An extensive history of Christian Science.

BRADEN, CHARLES S. *Christian Science Today: Power, Policy, Practice*. Dallas: Southern Methodist University Press, 1958. An objective work bringing the subject up to date.

OLMSTEAD. *HRUS*. Pp. 515-526.

SWEET. SRA. Pp. 375-378, 423, 424.

See Bibliography in Chapter 14 which applies to most of the cults discussed in this chapter.

22

CHALLENGES TO SUPERNATURAL RELIGION

THE CHURCHES in the United States were mainly orthodox in theology in 1865. But new trends, beginning to develop even before the conflict on slavery, were to produce the system of naturalistic religion called Liberalism. Several influences contributed to the rise of Liberalism by the end of the century.

Idealistic Philosophy

Immanuel Kant, the father of idealistic thought, in his *Critique of Practical Reason,* located the source of religion in the human breast rather than in a divine objective revelation from God in the Bible. His categorical imperative was in reality an assertion of ethical law in man's innate sense of the right by the operation of his conscience. This sense of value in man enabled one to posit the soul, God and immortality. The sense of the immanence of God in man or the possession of the "divine spark" by man enables him, with Christ as an example, to build a religious life without necessity for atonement by the death of Christ. The Bible, a book apart from the noumenal world of God and the soul, is thus nothing but a subjective record of man's religious experience and is only a part of the realm of phenomena which man knows by reason and sensation. This opened the way for an unabashed and destructive biblical criticism. The emphasis of Kant's follower Georg W. F. Hegel upon philosophical evolution as the process by which God was manifesting Himself in history in the development of what Hegel called freedom, led to optimism concerning man's ability to progress in the future. All these ideas will be recognized as elements of modern Liberalism.

Friedrich E. D. Schleiermacher, with his emphasis upon dependence as the essence of religion, made experience the basis of faith rather than the Bible and faith in Christ. Love to man after the example of Jesus was the core of religion. Albrecht Ritschl emphasized the practice of religion in community to achieve divinity after the example of Christ, who had become divine through His life of service. These views of the philosophers congealed into concepts of the fatherhood of God and the brotherhood of man so characteristic of Liberalism. These views were brought to America by such men as Josiah Royce (1855-1916) and others in influential positions in Harvard, Yale and other colleges. To such men the kingdom of God was to be the outcome of a natural evolution of the effort of churchmen in society through cooperation with God, rather than a cataclysmic affair which would be realized by the coming of Christ. This optimistic interpretation of history still lingers on the American theological scene despite the pessimism of Neo-orthodoxy and two world wars.

Horace Bushnell and the Rise of Liberal Religious Education

The writings of Horace Bushnell (1802-1876) were another influence, especially in the area of religious education, in the rise of Liberalism with its challenge to supernaturalism in religion. Bushnell's Arminian father, the influence of Coleridge's idealism, and his angry reaction to Puritan revivalism with its emphasis that the small child must know sin and experience a tortuous experience of conviction before conversion were major forces in the development of his ideas. During his long pastorate from 1833 in North Church in Hartford, Connecticut, he came to theological conclusions at variance with those of his denomination.

Bushnell gave two talks on Christian nurture before a group of Congregational ministers. These were published in 1846 by the Massachusetts Sabbath School Society, but were withdrawn when opposition to his ideas developed. *Christian Nurture* was issued in 1847, and the final revised edition was published in 1861. Bushnell argued in the first part of his book that a child should grow up in a Christian home as a child of the covenant with godly parents so that he would never know himself as being anything but a Christian. This idea of growth into grace clashed with the idea that a child must have a conversion crisis after which growth in grace could take place. The second part of his book gave many practical rules to help parents achieve this state for their children.

In his book *Vicarious Sacrifice* (1865) he taught the moral influence view of the atonement, which asserts that the influence of Christ's love shown in His death on the cross is sufficient to bring about a better life without any substitutionary connotations in that death. Bushnell seems to have had a Sabellian view of the Trinity, in which there were not three persons but only manifestations in three different relationships of Father, Son and Spirit.

His idea of the spiritual development of the child apart from conversion through Christian nurture in the home is the foundation, along with the emphasis of John Dewey upon education as experience, on which liberal religious education has been built. Nurture, not conversion, is the way to Christian experience of the child who is not naturally depraved. Bushnell's stress upon the role of the home and his suggestions to parents in *Christian Nurture* on how to have a Christian home are still useful to the Christian parent. It is also interesting to remember that he helped to create the fine park system of Hartford and to select the site of the University of California at Berkeley. But more than all, he helped to rationalize and deepen opposition to revivalism.

Evolution and Orthodoxy

Evolution was another influence in the decline of supernatural religion and the rise of Liberalism. Charles R. Darwin in his *On the Origin of Species by Means of Natural Selection* (1859) argued for continuity from the simplest form of life to the higher complex forms. This continuity he explained by the hypothesis of favorable variations to environment being passed on by natural selection until a new species emerged. His *Descent of Man* (1871) was an application of this theory to man. After 1871 his theory became widely known in America, and several leaders tried to popularize it and to reconcile it with orthodoxy.

John Fiske, both in his philosophic and historical writings and lectures, argued that evolution was God's method of action in the universe and that Americans had an important part to play in the evolution of a better world. Henry Drummond, who worked with Moody in this country, tried in his books to show that evolution and Christianity were not incompatible. Lyman Abbott (1835-1922), in his book *The Theology of an Evolutionist* (1897), his work as an editor and his sermons as pastor of Plymouth Church, sought to reconcile Christianity and evolution. To him evolution was the process by which God provided for progress in history and the eventual purification of man. Man was to be viewed as the product of development rather than as the climax of God's creation.

This dogma of biological evolution not only denied special creation with fixity of "kind" by its assertion of descent with change but was also applied analogically to religion in a way which promoted the rise of Liberalism. Sin was to be considered as only the clinging residual instinct of "the tiger and the beast" which man would gradually work out. The faith itself was looked upon as an evolution from the simple worship of a storm god by the Jews at Sinai to a more complex ethical faith propounded by the prophets and realized in word and life by Christ. The dogma of religious progress guaranteed through the church the final perfectibility of man in a postmillenial world. Thus the optimism stemming from the eighteenth century *Philosophes* was accredited by the biological concept of evolution and carried over into nineteenth century Liberalism.

Biblical Criticism and Liberalism

Kantian idealism limited the Bible to the subjective realm of phenomena. Thus reason has the right to study the Bible as any other historical work with the techniques of literary and historical criticism. The idea of evolution seemed to support the concepts of a progressive revelation from a simple Jewish faith to a spiritual, ethical and more complex religion which was the result of an evolutionary process. The spread of colonialism brought Europeans into contact with other sacred writings, such as the Koran. The application of literary criticism to historical documents by such men as Leopold von Ranke stimulated a similar approach to the biblical documents. The publication of various revisions of the Bible and the rise of modern speech translations also stimulated this questioning of the former authority of the Bible.

Jean Astruc in the eighteenth century was one of the first to divide the Pentateuch according to the use of the names of Jehovah and Elohim for God. This process of literary analysis was brought to a peak by the Graf-Wellhausen theory. The Pentateuch was looked upon as a mosaic of several sources and the work of various editors rather than being the work of Moses. Prophetic books, such as Isaiah, were split in time and authorship on stylistic grounds, and Daniel was denied prophetic utterance by dating his book in a later century. F. C. Baur dated the books of the New Testament by the application of Hegelian dialectic to them.

Legalistic writings, such as James, were given an early date; writings reflecting Pauline teachings of the antithesis of grace, such as Romans and Galatians, had to come later; and writings in which Baur thought law and grace were synthesized, such as those of Luke, must have been written last. Thus did philosophical theory take precedence over other data in this presentation. The end result was the development of the idea that the Bible was a subjective revelation of man's growing consciousness of God and contained the Word of God without being in all parts the objective Word of God. Religion became a matter of an immanent experience of God.

Proponents of such ideas ran into strong orthodox opposition and heresy trials occurred often during the latter part of the century. Charles A. Briggs, professor at Union Theological Seminary in New York, clashed with A. A. Hodge and B. B. Warfield of Princeton over biblical questions and over his denial of the inerrancy and inspiration of the Bible. Briggs's book *Biblical Study: Its Principles, Methods and History* (1883) brought on a series of trials for heresy before the Presbytery of New York and the General Assembly of the Presbyterian Church in the U.S.A. In 1893 he was suspended from the ministry of that church and became an Episcopalian minister.[1] Henry P. Smith of Lane Seminary in Cincinnati was tried for an attack on verbal inspiration of the Scriptures in 1893 and suspended from the ministry of the Presbyterian church. A like fate befell A. C. McGiffert. Other denominations had similar heresy trials as a part of the struggle between the conservatives and the liberals. Even Pope Pius X condemned modernism in the works of such Roman Catholics as Alfred Loisy and George Tyrrell. Perhaps the most famous case in the twentieth century was the trial of the Baptist minister Harry Emerson Fosdick by the presbytery which forced him out of the Presbyterian church he was serving and brought about the building of Riverside Church for him in New York.

This discussion has revealed that all these forces resulted in the development of the new theology of Liberalism by 1890. God is looked upon as immanent in man, who can, with God's help together with the use of reason and the example of Christ, make moral progress. Thus God works by natural law rather than by miracle, so that miracles come under suspicion, and are denied or more often explained as natural phenomena. Christ is an ex-

[1]Peter G. Mode, *Sourcebook and Bibliographical Guide to American Church History* (Menasha, Wis.: George Banta Publishing Co., 1921), pp. 660-664.

ample rather than the Son of God who saves sinful man by His atonement. He is God's Son by moral effort rather than by essence of being, and His death as a moral influence calls out our love as His life calls for our following His example. Man will make such progress on earth through the work of the church in preaching, social reform and other activities that Christ's return will come after a millennium. These views or similar expressions dominated the seminaries of America until the challenge of Neo-orthodoxy began to reveal their inadequacy. Attacks were brought against these views by such conservatives as A. A. Hodge, B. B. Warfield, Francis L. Patton, all of Princeton; John A. Broadus, a Baptist, and after World War I by J. Gresham Machen. Not content with a mere negative approach, the conservatives founded Bible schools, colleges and seminaries to replace those lost to the liberal forces. At present, Liberalism seems to have lost much of its force and is being replaced in the major denominations by the force of Neo-orthodoxy.

BIBLIOGRAPHY

BUSHNELL, HORACE. *Christian Nurture*. New Haven: Yale University Press, 1916. The source of many of the ideas of modern religious educators.

CHENEY, MARY A. *Life and Letters of Horace Bushnell*. New York: Harper & Brothers, 1880. Contains much source material.

CROSS, BARBARA M. *Horace Bushnell: Minister to a Changing America*. Chicago: University of Chicago Press, 1958. An able biography.

KENNEDY, GAIL (ed.). *Evolution and Religion*. Boston: D. C. Heath and Company, 1957.

OLMSTEAD. *HRUS*. Pp. 465-474.

SWEET. *SRA*. Pp. 342-344.

23

THE RISE OF SOCIAL CONSCIENCE

THE SLAVERY ISSUE was the first major social problem to confront the American churches, but from then on interest and action concerning temperance, prohibition and other social issues developed. Near the end of the nineteenth century many churchmen began to take an interest in economics and the related question of the welfare of the worker. This was fortunate in many ways, for the church was in process of losing the worker and forgetting that the gospel was relevant to all of life. Unionism and, in some cases, either evolutionary democratic socialism or even Marxian revolutionary socialism were beginning to attract some of the workers.

Organized labor emerged as an answer to the rise of great business corporations of the industrial revolution with their life-and-death power over the worker. Many of the leaders of these corporations in the Gilded Age subscribed to the gospel of wealth of Andrew Carnegie, who declared in 1889 that a higher standard of living was the inevitable result of free competition. Because survival of the fittest was a fact of life, the weak would suffer from the strong in the process of readjustment in society, but the overall results would benefit society as those with wealth used it as a trust for good ends. Businessmen such as John D. Rockefeller looked upon their money-making ability as a gift from God and their success as evidence of the blessing of God upon their enterprise.

The immigration of workers from central and southeastern Europe near the end of the century brought in a supply of people who were willing to work at much lower rates than the earlier Teutonic Protestant immigrants from western Europe. This helped to force already low wages, which had been far outstripped by the cost of living, still lower.

Flaunting of wealth by those who had become rich increased the worker's unhappiness and gave him further incentive to form labor organizations. For example, Bradley Martin gave a ball at the Waldorf-Astoria Hotel, which was redecorated like the Versailles palace. He appeared in a suit of armor inlaid with one hundred thousand dollars' worth of gold. This compared most unfavorably with a wage of two dollars for the ten-hour day of skilled labor.

Labor's only recourse was union to fight this concentration of economic power. The Knights of Labor came into being in Philadelphia in 1869, and by 1885 this organization had more than one hundred thousand members. Near the end of the century it declined and was replaced by the American Federation of Labor, organized in 1886 under the leadership of Samuel Gompers. It had half a million members by 1900. Panics in 1873 and 1893 and the use of force against labor in the 1892 Homestead strike and the 1894 Pullman strike in Chicago embittered relations between business and labor.

Many workers felt that the church was an upper middle-class pietistic and conservative institution with little interest in their problems since, in many cases, capitalists made large gifts to churches and seemed thus to control the church, which catered to them because of their wealth. Besides, the church seemed to have the salvation of the individual soul as its main aim and appeared to be uninterested in social and economic problems of the workers. With few exceptions middle-class churches were places where the worker did not seem to fit in comfortably. They seemed to the worker to represent too much the employer's viewpoint and outlook, except for certain organized charities, which only attacked the symptoms and not the causes of the worker's problems.

The rise of liberal theology with a de-emphasis on personal salvation and in increased interest in the social problems of the day helped to change the climate of opinion in the church toward labor. Educators, such as the economists Richard T. Ely and John R. Commons, the journalist Henry George and the futuristic novelist Edward Bellamy created an interest in the need of economic justice as a social implication of the gospel.

Several individuals contributed to the rise of an increased social consciousness within the church. They tended to see man not as a sinner but as a child of God with capacity for moral and social advance which would eventually bring the kingdom of God upon earth. Washington Gladden (1836-1918), pastor of a Congregational church in Columbus, Ohio, from 1882 to 1918, had been influenced by Horace Bushnell to view the church as a social force and religion as a matter of love for the most part. His earlier editorial work on the *Independent* led him to views which he proclaimed in several books. Because he thought competition was unchristian, he wanted cooperation between capital and worker. This, he thought, would only come if the worker had a stake in the business through profit-sharing plans. This, coupled with Christian love, would solve the problems of capital and labor. He was also a strong advocate of the right of labor to organize into unions. His spirit was well expressed in his beautiful hymn, "O Master, Let Me Walk with Thee."

In his book *Our Country* (1885), another Congregational pastor, Josiah Strong, stated that lust for power and wealth was corrupting the United States. Large accumulations of wealth by a few caused him great concern, and through his writings many other churchmen became aware of the problem. His book was the social reform equivalent of *Uncle Tom's Cabin*.

George D. Herron (1862-1925), who finally joined the Socialist party and helped Mrs. E. D. Rand organize the leftist Rand School of Social Sciences in New York, was a Congregationalist pastor and, after 1893, professor of applied Christianity at Grinnell College, Iowa. He thought that the church should take for its mission creation of a just social order with public ownership of production. He spread these ideas widely through lectures and a journal named *The Kingdom*, which he began to publish in 1894. By 1900 he had to a great extent given up his church connections for open espousal of socialism.

Charles Sheldon's (1857-1946) popular novel *In His Steps* (1897) pictured the impact upon a community of a church whose members asked for one year, "What would Jesus do?" before any action. The book helped to popularize the cause of practical and social Christianity. Millions of copies of the novel by this Topeka, Kansas minister were sold.

Walter Rauschenbusch (1861-1918), who wanted to be a missionary to India, in 1886 took the pastorate of a small Baptist church on the West Side of New York. Here he saw the results of poverty firsthand. He left in 1897 to become professor of New Testament and, shortly after that, professor of church history in the Colgate-Rochester Theological Seminary until his death in 1918. In 1892 he organized the Brotherhood of the Kingdom to further the cause of Christian involvement in the economic and social problems of society. Most of its members later became Christian socialists.

While he upheld the idea of original sin and personal regeneration, at least for a large part of his life, Rauschenbusch adopted
as his master idea the concept of the kingdom of God as a gradually evolving social order which would achieve social justice on
earth. His earliest book, *Christianity and the Social Crisis* (1907),
was a historical analysis of Christian social concern from the era
of the prophets to the early church. This book pointed up his
idea of the enmity between capitalism and Christianity. Christian love and cooperation must, he said, replace laissez-faire. In
his *Christianizing the Social Order* (1912) he pointed out that
Christian democracy was evident in such organizations as the
family and the church, but must be extended by the church to the
social and economic order by social action and legislation. His
A Theology for the Social Gospel (1917) was a presentation of
the theology of the Social Gospel. Sin was mainly conceived to
be social, corporate and impersonal. Only social and economic
reform along somewhat socialistic lines resulting in the collapse
of capitalism would bring about the kingdom of God. The coming
of World War I brought heartbreak to him because he saw in
it the triumph of evil.

His ideas found a ready home in the University of Chicago.
Men such as Shailer Mathews, Shirley Jackson Case, Graham
Taylor and others proclaimed them from university chair, public
platform and pulpit as the churches' answer to industrial society.

Rauschenbusch and his followers leaned too much to the idea
that sin was mainly environmental and was a result more of
imitation than of heredity. Preoccupation with social action led
them to neglect the personal, saving relationship of men to Christ,
which was after all the final commission of Christ to men. Their
eschatology was overly optimistic in the light of two world wars
and brutal ideological dictatorships of the right and left since
1919. The conservative elements in the churches could not support the Social Gospel for these reasons, and big business was
naturally in opposition to what was considered to be—and in some
cases was—socialism.

The influence of the Social Gospel was strongest in the Social
Creed of the Federal Council of Churches of Christ in America,
which was organized in 1908 and later merged in 1950 into the
National Council of Churches. Many of the major denominations
created departments of labor or social action to apply the gospel
to social problems.

The effects of World War I and the depression, the opposition of orthodox forces, and Neo-orthodoxy's critical analysis of Liberalism, the theological foundation upon which the Social Gospel rested, helped to bring about its decline. Neo-orthodoxy in its earlier forms emphasized the depravity of man and the discontinuity between secular history and sacred history. It denied man's ability to do anything other than to react existentially to Christ in the crisis in which he was brought to face Christ by the Holy Spirit, and this crisis thus made some part of the Bible become the Word of God to him.

Perhaps the church can (and there are signs of this) become the moral and spiritual conscience of the nation on political and economic issues and so train and inspire its members that they will, as Christian citizens, seek to deal with social evils. In all of this the church should not as the church become an organized pressure group nor seek political and economic advantage for itself. To do so would endanger that separation of church and state which has been so beneficial in the United States. This should not, however, become an excuse for inaction on the part of church members, who are citizens as well as Christians and who should oppose evil wherever and in whatever form it manifests itself.

BIBLIOGRAPHY

CARTER, PAUL A. *The Decline and Revival of the Social Gospel . . . 1920-1940*. Ithaca, N.Y.: Cornell University Press, 1956.

HOPKINS, CHARLES H. *The Rise of the Social Gospel in American Protestantism, 1865-1915*. New Haven: Yale University Press, 1940. A scholarly account of the origins and development of the Social Gospel.

OLMSTEAD. *HRUS*. Pp. 480-484, 489-494.

RAUSCHENBUSCH, WALTER. *Christianizing the Social Order*. New York: The Macmillan Co., 1919. An account of the need and plan for Christianizing society.

———. *Christianity and the Social Crisis*. Boston: Pilgrim Press, 1907. A study of the social aims and action of the prophets, Christ and the early church.

These two books by Rauschenbusch constitute the credo of the Social Gospel. See Chapter 15 for bibliography relating to the origins of the Social Gospel.

SWEET. *SRA*. Pp. 353-357.

24

THE CHALLENGE OF FOREIGN MISSIONS

CHRIST'S COMMISSION to preach the gospel throughout the world did not, except for Indian missions in North
America, penetrate the consciousness of the Protestant church
until the nineteenth century. The great missionary movement of
that century, which Latourette in three volumes of his great
seven-volume work on missions characterizes as the "great century" in missions, had its beginnings in the eighteenth century
revivals in England.

The Second Awakening in America and awareness of the movement in England helped to promote foreign missions here. Adoniram Judson went to England to see whether the efforts of
himself and his friends could be coordinated with the English
missionary movement. When this proved impossible, he and his
friends were able to persuade the Congregationalists to set up
the American Board of Commissioners for Foreign Missions,
which was soon followed by a Baptist board. The former was particularly successful in Hawaii. From these little brooks developed
the mighty river of missionary effort after 1865.

Factors Promoting Foreign Missions

The spirit of Manifest Destiny promoted the expansion of
the boundaries of the United States to its natural frontiers, the
Rio Grande in the South and the Pacific in the West. This
spirit, coupled with a sense of mission to spread Christianity and
culture, stimulated the rise of missionary enthusiasm and made
the winning of the world for Christ seem a real possibility.

Perhaps even more, the revivals of the nineteenth century provided idealism for missions. The social perfectionism which grew
out of them was not to be limited to America alone, because
pagan people also had souls which must be saved. This could
happen only through the work of foreign missionaries.

The Spanish-American War, which brought Cuba, Puerto Rico

and the Philippines under American control, awakened a deeper enthusiasm for missions as these backward people became our responsibility to convert, civilize and lead to independence as soon as they were ready for it. Perhaps, some thought, this was Providence giving Protestant United States an opportunity to advance the Christian cause and to end Spanish imperialism and Roman Catholic authoritarianism in these areas. President McKinley said as much to friends in stating that he prayed over the problem of what to do with these Spanish colonies after the war. Senator Beveridge stated his belief that God had chosen Americans to lead in "the regeneration of the world" and to provide civilization for less advanced people.

As the old evangelical postmillennialism of the nineteenth century gave way to premillennialism before World War I, missionary enthusiasm increased among more conservative groups, and large numbers of missionaries were sent out. Because such groups believed that the time before Christ's return was short, they felt the church must work hard and fast to preach the gospel to all nations.

Interdenominational Organization
for the Missionary Task

Students of the history of missions have noticed that cooperation among the missionaries in foreign lands preceded the rise of the ecumenical movement at home and stimulated the expansion of that movement in the homeland. A three-week meeting in 1886 at Mount Hermon School in Northfield, Massachusetts, in which two hundred fifty-one college and YMCA young people participated, resulted in one hundred promising to go to the mission field, of whom twenty-one went out very quickly. The meeting also led to the formation in 1888 of the Student Volunteer Movement, which became a great recruiting agency for missions under the leadership of John R. Mott. Its aim was the evangelization of the world in that generation. Between 1899 and 1914 it is credited with recruiting more than four thousand five hundred missionaries. In 1902 the Missionary Education Movement was founded to further missionary education in Protestant denominations. The Laymen's Missionary Movement was founded in New York in 1906 through the efforts of John B. Sleman, Jr., to promote the support of as well as interest in missions on the part of laymen.

The Foreign Missions Conference of North America, now a part of the National Council of Churches, came into being in

1893 to eliminate overlapping in work abroad and to allocate areas for missionary activity to different groups. The International Missionary Council, founded in 1921 as a result of interdenominational world missionary conferences, had a similar function on a larger scale. It merged with the World Council of Churches in 1961.

Since World War II conservative groups have assumed the larger share of the burden of missionary effort throughout the world. Of the nearly thirty-nine thousand missionaries in the world in 1958, about twenty-one thousand came from North America. Of these twenty-one thousand, well over half came from conservative groups. The Evangelical Foreign Missions Association, the missionary arm of the National Association of Evangelicals, had about four thousand five hundred on the field, and the Interdenominational Foreign Missions Association had about seven thousand on the field. The Foreign Missions Fellowship, affiliated with the Inter-Varsity Christian Fellowship, has helped to inspire zeal for missionary service on campuses in somewhat the way the Student Volunteer Movement did formerly. Such organizations have taken advantage of radio and the airplane to speed their work. The Wycliffe Translators have pioneered scientific linguistic work in many areas as a tool to get the Bible into the vernacular.

The American Church on the Mission Field

American missionary work, although begun long before 1865, expanded rapidly after that date into every part of the world. Evangelism was the major aim of such work; but medical, agricultural and educational missions were also promoted as means to an end, a favorable hearing for the gospel.

The Presbyterians in Syria provided what has become the American University in Beirut to raise the standards of life of the people in that area. The Congregationalists in Turkey, barred from evangelism, did educational work through Roberts College and the American College for Girls. Arabia became the mission field of the Reformed Church in America, and Samuel Zwemer, its great missionary statesman, did much to promote missions to Muslims. After the British East India Company was dissolved following the Sepoy Mutiny of 1857, American missionaries were welcomed by the British government. Agricultural missions under the leadership of Sam Higginbotham, a Presbyterian missionary, resulted in the founding of the famous school of agriculture at Allahabad. The work which Judson began in Burma was continued by the Baptists and later by the Methodists. Presbyterians developed a strong work in Thailand.

Although the Second Opium War forced China to admit missionaries after 1858, it was not until the end of the century that great missionary forces were deployed in evangelistic, medical and educational activity in that land. A most notable convert was Charles Soong, the father of the wives of Sun Yat-sen and Chiang Kai-shek. The Presbyterians have had singular success in Korea, and the church in that land is a vigorous representative of first century Christianity. After the American government forced Japan to open her land to western culture and missionaries in 1858, the American churches sent in missionaries. The Philippines were opened to American missions after 1899 as the first field in which missionary work was carried on under the American flag.

Because British and European agencies, whose governments dominated large colonial areas, were on the field so early, American missionaries were not present in Africa in great numbers until the twentieth century. Greater stability in Latin America after the middle of the last century led to an expansion of missionary effort in that area. It would seem, however, that the most extensive American missionary effort has been devoted to Asia. The greatest endeavor was put forth between the Spanish-American War in 1898 and our entrance into World War I in 1917.

Problems of Missions in the Twentieth Century

Since World War I, except for the more conservative groups, there has been a relative decline in the number of missionary candidates and in support of missionary effort within the larger denominations. The rise of Liberalism seems to have been a factor in this decline, because the attention of youth was diverted to social reform, the race problem and the attempt to bring about world peace. All missionary effort has also faced major problems on the field.

The Laymen's Foreign Missionary Inquiry was organized in 1930 and financed by John D. Rockefeller to send commissions to China, Japan and Burma to report what form missionary endeavor should take in the future. The report, *Rethinking Missions* (1932) made by the chairman, William E. Hocking, a Harvard philosophy professor, was critical of past missionary effort and recommended changes in motives and methods and organization of missions along liberal lines. Similarities between pagan religions and Christianity should be exploited to find a common ground in knowing God. Hendrik Kraemer in his book *The Christian Message in a Non-Christian World* (1938) criticized this sharply. According to the report, philanthropic, educational and social work were to be emphasized, and the union of all missionary effort under such bodies as the International Missionary Council was proposed.

A return to isolation and the problems of the depression of 1929 lessened American interest in and support of missions. Material gain after both World Wars I and II seems to have claimed the attention of many young people and retarded interest in missions. The disappearance of large-scale revivals until after World War II eliminated a major force in the success of missions before World War I. War itself brought dislocation of missionary effort and diversion of enthusiasm and funds to winning the war.

The rise of Afro-Asian nationalism with a frenzied drive for independence from Western imperialism, especially after World War II, and the resurgence of the Muslim, Confucian, Buddhist and other faiths in these lands made them antagonistic to missions, which they suspected of Western imperialism. Many of the new states, such as Turkey, became so anticlerical that even the Muslim faith was severely restricted in that land.

In some countries, such as Spain and Colombia, Roman Catholicism as the religion of the majority has harshly persecuted national Protestant Christians and done all in its power to eliminate the work of Protestant missionaries. Communism with its atheistic and materialistic outlook has closed the doors since World War II to missionary effort in many lands, such as China and eastern Europe.

In spite of these problems at home and abroad the church has continued to press its work in the areas where the door is still open to missions. Much of the burden of world missions has now fallen upon the shoulders of the American churches. It is to be hoped that they will meet this challenge triumphantly in the future.

BIBLIOGRAPHY

LATOURETTE, KENNETH S. *A History of the Expansion of Christianity.* 7 vols. New York: Harper & Brothers, 1937-1945. See Volumes V and VI for able accounts of the missionary activities of the churches of the United States.
OLMSTEAD. *HRUS.* Pp. 495-506, 554-556.
SWEET. *SRA.* Pp. 357-360, 415-417.

25

THE CHURCH IN TWO WORLD WARS

THE CHURCH was challenged by the social problems of slavery, injustice to the worker, and war between 1865 and 1917. It could not resist schism in the slavery issue, it adopted the Social Gospel in many of its branches in order to help the worker, and in World War I it was much more chauvinistic than it was in World War II.

The Church Supports Peace

The early church up to the time of the *rapprochement* between Christianity and the Roman Empire in the days of Constantine had opposed participation in military activities. It did this because in the Roman union of religion and state such activities involved pagan sacrifices and rites, and because war was looked upon as inimical to the spirit of the gospel. When Christianity became the state religion in 380, Christians took their place in the army as patriotic citizens. The partnership between church and state during the Reformation and the reformers' teaching of obedience to civil authority led to participation in war by the Christian. In fact, in nearly every state Protestantism was not established without the use of armed force by both Roman Catholics and Protestants. Only small groups, such as the Mennonites, who separated church and state, adopted the principle of nonresistance and became historic pacifists. They interpreted sections of the New Testament literally on this point. The Quakers took a similar stand in the seventeenth century, and the Moravians in the next century followed the same practice.

During the American Revolution these groups were neutral and willingly endured the persecution and suffering which came because of their stand. These historic pacifists, who take the New Testament abhorrence of war literally, must be distinguished from later almost professional pacifists of World War I and II.

During the nineteenth century, peace movements which were not pacifistic were organized in the United States. As early as 1815 David L. Dodge, a Presbyterian merchant in New York, organized a New York peace society to oppose war as inconsistent with religion. In that same year in Ohio and Massachusetts peace societies were organized. These and other state societies united to form the American Peace Society in 1828 because of the devoted efforts of William Ladd. They proposed arbitration and an international organization to solve problems that might lead to war; but the Mexican War and later the Civil War weakened their efforts.

The peace movement revived after 1865, and in 1889 the WCTU founded a department to devote part of its efforts to advancing the cause of peace and arbitration. In 1893 a Universal Peace Congress was held in Chicago. The American Association of Ministers came into being in 1902 to promote peace. The Carnegie Endowment for International Peace was founded with a ten-million-dollar endowment in 1910 to promote the cause of peace. The Hague Conferences of 1899 and 1907 adopted a court of arbitration and set up rules to humanize any war that might develop. All these endeavors helped to rejuvenate the American Peace Society and create an atmosphere of opposition to war in the United States when World War I started in 1914. Charles W. Eliot of Harvard and Nicholas Murray Butler of Columbia in the field of education, and President Wilson in government supported the peace movement.

This climate of opinion gradually changed after 1914. The churches supported Wilson's neutrality policy and wanted the United States to be a peacemaker. Aid to the innocent sufferers in war through the Red Cross found ready support. Because the British had control of the cables from Europe, stories of terrible German atrocities were relayed to America. Public opinion, especially after release of the Zimmerman note promising Mexico part of the Southwest if she would enter the war on the side of Germany, turned against Germany and in favor of arming America so that she might help to enforce a just peace. Gradually the country, especially the East, shifted toward intervention. After the sinking of the *Lusitania* by a German submarine, the country, the churches and the religious press, which reflected these shifting positions, were ready for Wilson's war to make the world safe for democracy and to end war once and for all.

The Church in World War I

The churches loyally supported the war and resolutions were passed in church bodies such as the Episcopal and the Methodist to assure the government of their support of the war effort. All the traditional activities of a church in war were carried on. Chaplains were provided to care for the spiritual needs of the soldiers. Red Cross units could count on church people to roll bandages and provide support for their work. The YMCA was able, through public generosity, to set up canteens and reading rooms at the front for the soldiers. The American Bible Society provided Bibles for every soldier.

Unfortunately, much of the support of war by the churches went beyond the traditional bounds mentioned above. Such leaders as Newell Dwight Hillis of Plymouth Congregational Church, Brooklyn, preached hatred of the Germans as almost subhuman beings. He and others used the pulpit to spread atrocity stories, later proved to be untrue, to recruit soldiers and to sell war bonds to the public. German music was banned, and many people changed their German names because of the hatred of all things German which had been whipped up by large-scale government propaganda. Pacifist opponents of war faced difficulty both from the government and the public. Although historic peace groups, such as the Mennonites and Quakers, were exempted from military service, many were put in prison camps. Pacifist ministers were held up to ridicule, prosecuted in court, and in some cases even suffered bodily assault.

Interchurch cooperation during the war and the ability to raise great sums of money by coordinated interdenominational effort stimulated postwar cooperation to raise money for spiritual projects. The Methodists proposed to raise forty million dollars, and had that amount oversubscribed. Other groups had similar success. The Interchurch World Movement was set up to survey the needs of missions and the resources of the church, and to create and raise a budget to meet these needs; but it was not successful. The churches also cooperated after the war in the temperance movement which added the Eighteenth Amendment to the Constitution.

Postwar Pacifism

Although the churches learned the value of cooperation in the war, the idealism with which they entered the war was shattered by the end of the war, and a new peace movement developed which was much more aggressive and united in its distrust of armaments and war. This disillusionment was increased by the revisionist historians' revelations of the untrustworthiness of the statements issued by nations at the beginning of the war blaming each other for the war. It was increased too by the special senatorial Nye Committee which, after investigating the munitions industry in 1934 and 1935, found considerable evidence that the armament industry had helped to bring about the war. And worse, it had often traded impartially with both sides through neutrals. In addition, the decade of hope for peace through international cooperation after 1919 gave way, with the onset of depression and the rise of dictators by 1929, to a decade of despair, in which each nation sought its own solution for problems of peace and prosperity.

For these reasons a strong antiwar movement developed among religious groups. When *The World Tomorrow* polled fifty-three thousand Protestant ministers in 1931, of the nearly twenty thousand replies more than three-fifths disapproved of any future war and slightly more than one-half would have nothing to do with such war. Theologically liberal professional pacifism seemed to be the order of the day in several denominations, while the historic pacifists, such as the Mennonites and Quakers, were strengthened in their opposition to war under any circumstances and in support of disarmament. The *Christian Century* represented this liberal pacifist and noninterventionist viewpoint.

Between 1939 and 1941, when war broke out and when America entered it, a great reversal took place. Men like Reinhold Niebuhr in *Christianity and Crisis* argued for intervention by the United States because, while both sides were sinful, one was relatively more sinful than the other and would destroy civilization if not defeated. The Japanese attack at Pearl Harbor in December, 1941, convinced many of these liberal pacifists of the necessity of war. But to the credit of the church it did not sanctify World War II as a great crusade. The church moved from favoring pacifism to preparedness and at last to war.

The Church in World War II

Although they did not sanctify the war as a crusade, recruit soldiers or sell bonds, the churches loyally supported the war effort in the standard fashion of past wars. The churches gave more help to the approximately eight thousand sincere conscientious objectors assigned to noncombatant service in work camps and to those who, for reasons of conscience, refused to register for selective service and were imprisoned for their refusal. Two-thirds of the eight thousand were from the historic pacifist churches and the rest were liberal pacifists. The churches also helped to provide chaplains in a ratio of one for one thousand two hundred men. The social and recreational work of such agencies as the YMCA and the Knights of Columbus was done at home and abroad by over eleven hundred clubs of the United Service Organizations. Bibles and Testaments were distributed to the armed forces by many religious groups. Churches also helped refugees from totalitarianism to relocate in this land. The dislocation of missionary effort by the loss of European personnel was met by American aid and missionaries in many cases.

The churches also supported plans for a just and durable peace, and under the leadership of John Foster Dulles the Six Pillars of Peace were made the report of nearly four hundred delegates at a meeting in 1942 of the Federal Council of Churches' peace study commission. Churches at the end of the war set up restoration funds to raise over one hundred million dollars to pay for the restoration of churches and manses and to provide libraries for pastors in war-ravaged areas.

One can be thankful that the churches realized in World War II that their function precluded the recruiting of soldiers, the selling of war bonds and the preaching of hate. Instead, they gave spiritual aid to those in the armed forces, provided for the needy, and planned for a just and durable peace. This was more in keeping with the spiritual function of the church. But war is still an item of unfinished business for the church, which can point out the evils of war and foster world understanding.

BIBLIOGRAPHY

ABRAMS, RAY H. *Preachers Present Arms.* New York: Round Table Press, 1933. The best account of how the church engaged in World War I as a "holy crusade."
———. (ed.). "The Churches and the Clergy in World War II," *Annals of the American Academy of Political and Social Science.* Vol. 256 (March, 1948), 110-119. An able dicussion of the works of mercy of the church in World War II.
OLMSTEAD. *HRUS.* Pp. 506-514, 565-572.
SWEET. *SRA.* Pp. 391-406, 428-438.

26

PROTESTANT COOPERATION
AND REUNION

THE PROTESTANT CHURCHES of the United States before 1865 seemed to be bent more on schism and disintegration than on cooperation and reunion or integration. After the successful struggle to preserve the Union, a trend toward interdenominational cooperation and later organic reunion and confederation became evident about 1880. Perhaps the common struggle to deal with major urban social problems, the tendency to large-scale organization after 1865, the theological indifferentism created by Liberalism, which stressed life above doctrine and cooperation on the mission field, may have stimulated this trend. Such cooperation and unity began first with nondenominational and interdenominational cooperation. It was later manifested in several organic reunions of like and unlike denominations, while at the same time a movement toward local, national and international confederations developed. (See diagram at end of chapter.)

Cooperative Movements Among the Churches

Cooperation by different churches had been evidenced early in the joint efforts during the Second Awakening in the conduct of camp meetings, such as that at Cane Ridge in 1801, when the burden of ministry was shared by those of different denominations. The Presbyterians and Congregationalists united in the Plan of Union in 1801 to carry on mission work in the West, and the American Board of Commissioners for Foreign Missions carried on the joint work of several Calvinistic bodies. The American Bible Society, the American Tract Society and the American Sunday-School Union early in the nineteenth century brought the denominations together in cooperative work. The YMCA and its United States Christian Commission, created during the Civil War, provided areas of cooperation. The Christian Endeavor

Movement and the Student Volunteer Movement inspired the youth of several denominations to work together.

Since 1914 many new organizations in which people of different denominations cooperate have come into being. The Religious Education Association of 1903 under the leadership of William R. Harper gave way in 1922 to the International Council of Religious Education, which coordinated the educational work among youth of more than forty denominations. It tended to put technique above content. Conservative groups have also cooperated in the work of such organizations as Youth for Christ International, Child Evangelism Fellowship and the Christian Service Brigade, an organization similar to the Boy Scouts but with a religious as well as ethical, social and recreational program.

This trend has been especially pronounced in missionary work. The Foreign Missions Conference of North America of 1893 helped to inspire the founding of the International Missionary Council in 1921, to coordinate the missionary work of the churches so that duplication of effort might be avoided by comity arrangements in the mission fields of the world. In 1945 the National Association of Evangelicals set up the Evangelical Foreign Missions Association to provide services to missionaries of conservative persuasion. By 1958 it was serving the interests of nearly four thousand five hundred missionaries, more than a fifth of all missionaries from North America. The Interdenominational Foreign Missions Association by 1958 was serving nearly seven thousand missionaries from North America who belong to "faith" boards. Thus in these different ways denominations have cooperated increasingly to achieve common ends by organizations for joint interest.

Organic Reunion of Churches

Organic reunions of denominations of *similar* theological backgrounds and polity have increased in numbers during the twentieth century and especially since World War I. The Old and New School groups in the North reunited in 1869 to form the Presbyterian Church in the United States of America, and in 1906 part of the Cumberland Presbyterian Church merged with the union of 1869. Some abstained from this merger to form a continuing Cumberland Presbyterian Church. In 1958 the United Presbyterian Church united with the large organization to form the United Presbyterian Church, U.S.A. The Methodists of the North and South ended their long schism over slavery in 1939 when they united at Kansas City to form the Methodist Church. Several reunions of Lutherans have occurred and more are under way. The United Lutheran Church of 1918 was the result of reunion of the General Synod, the General Council, and the United Synod of the South, which were the major descendants of colonial German Lutheranism. In 1930 the Ohio, Texas, Iowa and Buffalo Synods reunited to form the American Lutheran Church. American Lutheran and Evangelical Lutheran churches united in 1960 to form The American Lutheran Church. In 1963 the Lutheran Church in America came into being, consisting of the old United Lutheran Church, Suomi Synod, American Evangelical Lutheran Church, and the Augustana Lutheran Church. The Northern Baptist Convention, as it gave up many Calvinistic ideas, reunited with the Arminian Free Baptist churches in 1911 in what has been known since 1950 as the American Baptist Convention. It has lost many congregations to the Conservative Baptist Association and the General Association of Regular Baptists. Many other reunions have occurred among smaller bodies with like theology and polity.

Unions have also occurred between churches of *unlike* theology and polity. The union of Congregational and Christian churches in 1931 to form the Congregational Christian Churches is an early illustration of such a union in the United States. This body in turn united with the Evangelical and Reformed Church in 1957 to form the two-million-member United Church of Christ. Even larger mergers have occurred in Canada, India and the Philippines. The Congregational, Methodist, and a large part of the Presbyterian churches in Canada united in 1925 to form the United Church of Canada. This trend may be expected to continue because of various statements by influential leaders and the organization of committees and the submission of resolutions aimed at creating union of some of the larger denominations.

Local, National and International Confederation

The constituent units in organizations across denominational lines have up to the present retained sovereignty and freedom of action to accept or reject the proposals of the body in which they cooperate. Thus organizations of this type should technically be known as confederations rather than federations, because they do not permit any loss of their sovereignty to the central organization.

National confederations have been formed to allow denominations to cooperate in matters of common interest. The Open and

Institutional Church League of 1894 was the first step in the founding of the Federal Council of the Churches of Christ in America. A conference at Carnegie Hall in New York in 1905 drafted a constitution for the Federal Council, which came into being at a meeting in Philadelphia in 1908. Unlike the American Evangelical Alliance of 1867, which had a strong creedal statement, the constitution[1] had little to say on this point beyond faith in Christ as "Divine Lord and Saviour." More interest was shown in a fourteen-point Social Creed of the Churches which committed the Council to a program along the lines of the Social Gospel. The Federal Council cooperated with state and city confederations.

In 1950 at Cleveland the Federal Council changed its name to the National Council and became a larger organization with which such bodies as the Foreign Missions Conference of North America and the International Council of Religious Education merged. These became departments of the National Council of Churches. It represents more than thirty denominations, some of them the largest Protestant bodies, with over forty million people. But the Missouri Synod and the Southern Baptist Convention have been among the largest of the groups so far to refuse cooperation.

Conservative groups were not to be left out of this process. In 1941 the American Council of Christian Churches, led by Carl McIntire, came into being. This group will admit to membership only those denominations which have no tie with the National Council, which they consider to be apostate and socialistic. The National Association of Evangelicals began in 1943 with the adoption of a constitution drawn up in St. Louis in 1942. Like the American Council it has a strong creedal statement, but unlike it the National Association of Evangelicals will permit churches, denominations and individuals to hold membership even though they belong to organizations which support or have links with the National Council of Churches. Still another group is the smaller Independent Fundamental Churches of America. The NAE, which is the largest of these organizations, claims a membership of two million and service to over ten million Protestants.

International confederation has proceeded along two lines and, in both, Americans have provided most of the leadership and

[1]Peter G. Mode, *Sourcebook and Bibliographical Guide to American Church History* (Menasha, Wis.: George Banta Publishing Co., 1921), pp. 669-671.

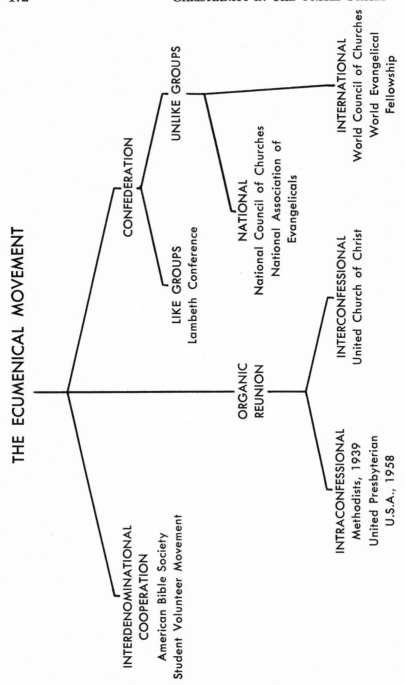

THE ECUMENICAL MOVEMENT

INTERDENOMINATIONAL
COOPERATION
American Bible Society
Student Volunteer Movement

CONFEDERATION

LIKE GROUPS
Lambeth Conference

UNLIKE GROUPS

NATIONAL
National Council of Churches
National Association of
Evangelicals

INTERNATIONAL
World Council of Churches
World Evangelical
Fellowship

ORGANIC
REUNION

INTRACONFESSIONAL
Methodists, 1939
United Presbyterian
U.S.A., 1958

INTERCONFESSIONAL
United Church of Christ

financial support. Episcopalians throughout the world have met in conference about every ten years since 1867, when the first Lambeth Conference was held. The World Alliance of Reformed Churches was organized in 1875 and held its first meeting in 1877. The World Methodist Council was organized in 1881. The International Congregational Council began in 1891, and the Baptist World Alliance began in 1905. Lutherans have cooperated in the Lutheran World Federation since 1923.

But international confederation has also crossed denominational lines. The Evangelical Alliance, an organization of individuals, which was founded in London in 1846 with an American branch in 1867, had a strong evangelical creedal statement and an emphasis on prayer and evangelism. It has since been replaced by the less creedal World Council of Churches, which was founded in 1948 at Amsterdam by representatives of more than one hundred thirty denominations from about forty countries. International conferences of missions at regular intervals since that at Edinburgh in 1910, those on life and work since that at Stockholm in 1925, and on faith and order beginning with the meeting at Lausanne in 1927, financed by J. P. Morgan, all have contributed to the creation of the World Council. American leadership and money had a leading part in this ecumenical movement. The second meeting of the World Council was held at Evanston in 1954 and another meeting took place at New Delhi in 1961.

Evangelicals have also organized international confederations. The American Council led in the formation of the International Council of Christian Churches at Amsterdam in 1948. Through the efforts of leaders of the National Association of Evangelicals, the World Evangelical Fellowship was founded in Holland in 1951. Both groups have opposed what they believe are tendencies toward a superchurch on both the national and international levels by the National Council and the World Council. Certainly any organization which destroys the unity of the spiritual organism, the invisible Church, will be a mistake. There is no doubt, however, that the trend to reunion and ecumenicity will continue and perhaps even intensify in rapidity.

BIBLIOGRAPHY

OLMSTEAD. HRUS. Pp. 403, 404, 527-540.
SWEET. SRA. Pp. 339, 340, 387-390, 424-427, 438-441, 451-453.

History of Ecumenicity:

GOODALL, NORMAN. *The Ecumenical Movement.* London: Oxford University Press, 1961. An able presentation of the history and work of the World Council of Churches.

McINTIRE, CARL. *Twentieth Century Reformation.* Collingswood, N.J.: Christian Beacon Press, 1946.

MURCH, JAMES D. *Cooperation Without Compromise* . . . Grand Rapids: Wm. B. Eerdmans Publishing Co., 1956. An able account of the founding and work of the National Association of Evangelicals.

PACHE, RENÉ. *The Ecumenical Movement.* Dallas: Dallas Theological Seminary, 1950. A conservative reaction to and history of the ecumenical movement.

RIAN, EDWIN H. *The Presbyterian Conflict.* Grand Rapids: Wm. B. Eerdmans Publishing Co., 1940. The story of the fundamentalist-liberal clash in the Presbyterian Church in the United States of America.

ROUSE, RUTH, and NEILL, STEPHEN C. (eds.). *A History of the Ecumenical Movement, 1517-1948.* London: Society for Promoting Christian Knowledge, 1954. A comprehensive treatment of the ecumenical movement to 1948.

SLOSSER, GAIUS J. (ed.). *Christian Unity, Its History and Challenge in All Communions.* New York: E. P. Dutton & Co., 1929.

27

THE RETURN TO ABSOLUTISM

RELIGIOUS LIBERALISM seemed to have triumphed by 1914, but by 1919 its basic tenets were increasingly under challenge, although its effects lingered on. A study of the religious beliefs of five hundred ministers in the Chicago area and of two hundred students in five geographically separate seminaries in 1929 by G. H. Betts demonstrated that about a quarter of the ministers but more than two-thirds of the students rejected the New Testament as an infallible rule of faith and practice. Over half of the ministers and 95 percent of the students rejected the account of creation in Genesis. One-third of the ministers and slightly more than three-quarters of the students rejected miracles. These statistics help to demonstrate the erosion that Liberalism—with its idea of an immanent God, a human Christ, a moral influence or example theory of the atonement, a view of sin as the result of the imitation of Adam rather than a heritage from him, a Bible which only contained the Word of God, and a future guaranteed by the Social Gospel—had brought about in the leadership of the churches. It seemed that the humanistic philosophy of the Renaissance and Enlightenment had conquered, and a shallow sentimental optimism seemed to be the order of the day.

Since 1914, the experience of two world wars, the rise of rightist Nazi or Fascist types of totalitarianism and its leftist Communist equivalents, and the soul-searing experiences of the great depression of 1929 have increasingly led to a pessimism in which men have returned in some measure to theologies with absolutist roots. This tendency has been manifested in what was often called Fundamentalism, Neo-orthodoxy, Neo-Thomism and the rise of many absolutist cults, such as the Oxford Group or, as it is now known, Moral Rearmament. The jazz age of the twenties has given way to much more sober consideration of man's origin, purpose for being and future destiny. Supernaturalism and absolutism began to replace the relativistic theology of Liberalism with its roots in German idealism.

The Conservative Reaction to Liberalism

This conservative attack on Liberalism took both negative and positive forms. The Scopes trial in Dayton, Tennessee, in 1925 was an attempt, with William Jennings Bryan representing the conservatives and Clarence Darrow representing the liberals, to uphold the state law banning the teaching of evolution in the public schools. The evolutionist John T. Scopes lost his case.

Similarly in church bodies attempts were made to root out liberals. Perhaps the most spectacular instance of this was the conflict of the popular Baptist minister Harry Emerson Fosdick (1878–) with the Presbyterians, because of his liberal sermons in the First Presbyterian Church in New York, where he was a stated supply from 1919. His 1922 sermon "Shall the Funda-mentalists Win?" brought the issue of his liberalism before the General Assembly of the church in 1923, and Fosdick resigned in 1924 to become pastor of the famous Riverside Church, which was built for him.

Conservative Presbyterians opposed the Auburn Affirmation of 1923, which was signed by nearly one thousand three hundred ministers by 1924, with its protest against making belief in the virgin birth, Christ's miracles, an inerrant Bible, substitutionary atonement and the physical resurrection of Christ a doctrinal test for Presbyterian ministers. The able J. Gresham Machen, a pro-fessor in Princeton Seminary, upheld the conservative position in his writings and organized an independent mission board which was to be free of liberals. When his denomination demanded that he cease to support the independent board, he and his followers left the Presbyterian Church U.S.A. and founded Westminster Seminary in Philadelphia in 1929. In 1936, they formed another Presbyterian body, which was renamed the Orthodox Presbyterian Church in 1939.

The Baptists also had their divisions, but the looser polity al-lowed the conservative wing to remain in the church and to found the more conservative Eastern Baptist Theological Semi-nary in 1925. Some did leave the Northern Baptist Convention (later named the American Baptist Convention) to found the General Association of Regular Baptists in 1933, and others later created the Conservative Baptist Association in 1947.

The conservatives were not satisfied with these negative tactics but engaged in positive action against Liberalism even before World War I. The Niagara Bible Conference in 1895 defined the five essentials of the faith as a verbally inerrant Bible, the virgin birth and deity of Christ, the substitutionary atonement, the physical resurrrection, and the bodily second coming of Christ. The doctrines of the Niagara Conference became the rallying cry of many conservatives, some of whom were extremely militant.

Literature upholding this theological position as well as attacking Liberalism was produced. The oil money of Lyman and Milton Stewart financed the founding of the Bible Institute of Los Angeles and the Stewart Evangelistic Fund to reprint W. E. Blackstone's *Jesus is Coming*. They also gave three hundred thousand dollars for the publication of the twelve-volume paperback set called *The Fundamentals*, beginning in 1909 under the successive editorship of A. C. Dixon, Louis Meyer and R. A. Torrey. About three million separate volumes were given free to ministers, theological professors and students, YMCA and YWCA secretaries and Sunday school superintendents. Articles by scholarly conservatives, such as W. H. Griffith Thomas, James Orr, Robert E. Speer and Howard A. Kelly, stated the fundamentals of the faith and the need of evangelism and missions, and attacked evolution, biblical criticism and modern cults. J. Gresham Machen in scholarly books, such as *The Origin of Paul's Religion* (1921) and *The Virgin Birth of Christ* (1930), upheld the conservative position on these points. Robert Dick Wilson in his *A Scientific Investigation of the Old Testament* and other writings furthered the conservative program. This scholarly tradition has been carried on by the widely circulated magazine *Christianity Today*, under the editorship of Carl F. H. Henry, and also by a growing theological literature by conservative writers. Merrill Tenney, Carl Henry and Gleason Archer, Jr. are among the outstanding conservative writers of our day.

The conservatives took action to found Bible institutes, colleges and seminaries which would be true to their viewpoint. The Missionary Training Institute of Nyack, founded by A. B. Simpson in 1882, and Moody Bible Institute, which Moody brought into being in 1886, became centers for biblical training. Many schools, such as Wheaton College, Gordon College, and Asbury College, support the conservative position. Seminaries, such as Westminster, Dallas, and Fuller, have taken a stand for conservative theology. Although such institutions take this stand, they are more irenic than the "fundamentalists" of the twenties.

The resurgence of mass evangelism in the fifties must also be noted. Youth for Christ International has specialized in reaching youth with Saturday night rallies, and Young Life and other groups are trying to reach high school young people with the gospel. Child Evangelism Fellowship seeks to help evangelize younger children. Mass evangelism in the Moody tradition has been carried on all over the world by Billy Graham, and Charles A. Fuller has sought to do the same thing over the radio.

Neo-orthodoxy Challenges Liberalism

Neo-orthodoxy recognized that naively optimistic Liberalism had no answer for the demonic in history as manifested in two brutal total world wars and rightist and leftist totalitarianism. It denied the liberal view that the environment was the source of sin, which was a matter of imitation rather than heredity. The Social Gospel also had not adequately dealt with this problem of personal sin. Moreover, people were disenchanted with a Liberalism rooted in a Kantian idealism which found the roots of religion in the human breast.

The Neo-orthodox movement stems from the Danish thinker Kierkegaard and has been developed through the work of Karl Barth (1886–). Barth was trained as a liberal, wrote for a religious liberal German magazine and became a seminary professor in various German seminaries until the Nazis forced him to move to Basel, Switzerland, where he taught and now writes. He emphasizes the utter discontinuity between God and man. God is other than man and transcendent and holy. This leads Barth and others to differentiate between secular history and holy history and thus cut God off from history.

Most of Barth's followers look upon the Bible as a book which by the Holy Spirit's activity in the individual heart becomes the Word of God to the individual, although it is not objectively and historically the Word of God. For this reason the Neo-orthodox readily accept the findings of biblical criticism as do the liberal. Sin is universal, but the account of the origin of sin in Genesis is usually treated as a myth which, however, is said to enshrine the historical fact that there is sin in the world. The eschatological end to human history is divorced from and beyond history. Usually, with exceptions, such as Reinhold Niebuhr, there is not much interest in social action as the responsibility of the church. Although Neo-orthodoxy has stimulated a return to biblical theology among formerly liberal theologians, it is at odds with historic Christianity in spite of Barth's idea that he was reviving Calvinism. Emil Brunner holds similar views, but disagrees with Barth in his insistence that God can be known partially in nature and that the image of God in man is not completely lost.

Reinhold Niebuhr (1892–) has become the chief American exponent of Neo-orthodoxy. His pastorate in Detroit between 1915 and 1928 among auto factory workers led him to give more attention to social and economic problems. From his chair at Union Theological Seminary in New York he has lectured and written on his views. To him, sin is pride and selfishness. When God encounters man, this can be overcome, and man under God can choose and achieve relative good in a sinful and complex society. In this way he links the older view of sinful man with social reform and tries to mediate between Barth's pessimism and the old optimism of the liberal Social Gospel.

Princeton Seminary, with Otto Piper and for a time Emil Brunner as professors, also became a center of Neo-orthodoxy in the United States. Paul Tillich (1886–), a German refugee who taught at Union Theological Seminary and is now at Harvard University, is another exponent of Neo-orthodox thinking. Others, such as Edwin Lewis of Drew Seminary, Wilhelm Pauck and Nels Ferré may be counted as leading exponents of these ideas, which have been widely adopted in America since 1930.

Neo-orthodoxy has stimulated a return to the study of biblical theology and to the consciousness of man's sin and his need of a sovereign, transcendent God who reaches down to him. But it has retained Liberalism's critical view of the Scriptures.

Roman Catholic Absolutism

Etienne Gilson and Jacques Maritain have brought about a revival of interest in the work of Thomas Aquinas, which became the definitive theology of the Roman Catholic church at the Council of Trent. They and other scholars have tried to adapt it to the problems of science and a complex society. The Roman Catholic church condemned its liberals, such as the French scholar Loisy and the British thinker Tyrrell, and both were excommunicated from the church. Thus the old absolutist theology seems to have emerged triumphant in the Roman Catholic church.

One wonders, with all this reversion to absolutism in theology among the conservatives, Neo-orthodox and Roman Catholics, whether there is not so much a revival of religion as a revival of interest in religion. There seems to be a tendency to institutionalize and popularize religion. It is the vogue to be religious, and politicians, newspapers and magazines stress it. Well over one hundred million people in America are identified with religious groups. The wide sale of peace of mind books, such as those of the Jewish writer Joshua Liebman, the Roman Catholic Fulton J. Sheen and the Protestant Billy Graham, attest the desire for peace in the present as we face our time of troubles, before which man seems to be so helpless. Norman Vincent Peale seems to be the apostle of a cult of reassurance. There is some evidence that the Christian religion may become an American folk religion emasculated of the doctrinal content which gives it real vitality. If it becomes a religion of faith in faith rather than faith in God, it will not be adequate to meet the challenge of the times.

BIBLIOGRAPHY

COLE, STEWART G. *The History of Fundamentalism*. New York: R. R. Smith, 1931. An older but less objective work than that of Furniss.

FURNISS, NORMAN F. *The Fundamentalist Controversy 1918-1931*. New Haven: Yale University Press, 1954. A scholarly account of the fundamentalist movement.

GASPER, LOUIS. *The Fundamentalist Movement*. The Hague: Mouton & Co., 1963.

HENRY, CARL F. H. *Fifty Years of Protestant Theology*. Boston: W. A. Wilde Co., 1950. An able conservative account of recent theological trends.

HORDERN, WILLIAM. *A Layman's Guide to Protestant Theology*. New York: The Macmillan Co., 1955. An able survey from a somewhat liberal theological viewpoint.

NASH, RONALD H. *The New Evangelicalism*. Grand Rapids: Zondervan Publishing House, 1963.

LIGHTNER, ROBERT P. *Neo-evangelicalism*. Findlay, Ohio: Dunham Publishing Co., 1962.

OLMSTEAD. *HRUS*. Pp. 474, 547-553, 572-583.

SWEET. *SRA*. Pp. 406-410, 417-421, 450, 451.

28

CONTINUING PROBLEMS IN THE AGE OF CONFLICT SINCE 1917

THE PROBLEM of the relationship of the Christian to the society about him has been a perennial concern of the church. During the nineteenth century the churches seemed to think that evangelism and individual action by each Christian would bring about a perfect world order through the efforts of Christians. This movement reached its peak in the Social Gospel just before 1914. World Wars I and II and the economic problems of the depression of 1929 as well as the problems of the rising tide of totalitarianism since 1919 brought disillusion and doubt as to how far the church can conquer the world. This expressed itself in the conservative adherence to the idea that evangelization is the church's main function and in the Neo-orthodox pessimism concerning secular history as an area of divine action. Perhaps a newer, more chastened view is emerging in which the function of the church is conceived as mainly spiritual and evangelistic. The individual Christian addresses himself to the problems of society in which the church as an organization does not participate lest it endanger our historic separation of church and state. With this as a backdrop, a brief consideration of continuing problems facing the Christian is in order.

The Christian and Intoxicating Beverages

The presence of more than five million alcoholics in the United States and the damage to life and property by auto accidents caused by intoxication indicate that the use of alcoholic beverages is a real social problem. The alliance of liquor interests with politics, and the realization by big business leaders that liquor created a problem of safety and efficiency in production, helped to create the prohibition movement to amend the Constitution at the end of World War I. Wartime prohibition to save grain for food seemed to justify continuance of this activity.

Unlike the Roman Catholic church, which took no stand on the issue, Protestant churches, particularly the Methodist and the Baptist, joined with the WCTU and the Anti-Saloon League to prohibit the sale and use of liquor. Prohibition was in effect in thirty-three states by 1918. Effort until our entry into World War I went into creating pressure by education for political action by temperance organizations and the churches. The Eighteenth Amendment was adopted by Congress in 1917 and went into effect in 1920. While this cut the consumption of liquor drastically for several years, desire of many for it led to political corruption and bootlegging; and the forces which effected prohibition forgot that legislation was only a part of the fight in which honest law enforcement was essential. Thus in 1933 the Eighteenth Amendment was repealed. But it is still true that modern methods of transportation and communication do not mix well with intoxicants and that liquor has become a grave social evil. A minimum step would at least be controls on advertising and regulation of the sale of liquor.

The Christian and Tension in Race Relations

Postwar fear of Communism and the status of the Negro created a strong spirit of nationalism which manifested itself in a hunt for Reds and in action by the Ku-Klux Klan against the Negroes. The modern form of the Ku-Klux Klan came into being in Georgia in 1915 under the leadership of William J. Simmons. By 1925 Edward Clarke's publicity campaign had won more than four million adherents in its fight against Roman Catholics, Negroes and others. Many Protestants were in its membership, which fought against the election of Roman Catholic Al Smith to the presidency in 1928, but its influence soon waned.

Since the twenties, progress has been slowly made in the fight to destroy racial discrimination against the nearly twenty million Negroes in the United States. It was eliminated in the armed services of the country during the fifties, and progress is now being made in government, business and the churches in this regard. Desegregation in education in the South is also gradually making headway, but there is still room for much effort on the part of Christians to end discrimination.

The Churches and Prosperity

Although ministers fought it with every means at their disposal, a decreasing influence of the church in organized society seems to have occurred after both world wars with the advent of postwar prosperity. Church attendance as a matter of social conformity, nonattendance at Sunday evening and midweek prayer services, the marked decline in family devotions, Sunday recreation, burial from funeral homes rather than from the church, and the rise of a secular spirit testify to this fact.

This spiritual decline with a corresponding de-emphasis on theology was coupled with an increasing prosperity in which the churches shared until 1929. Churches and church colleges over-built and overextended their credit. Massive cathedral-like churches with divided chancels were built. Since World War II Gothic architecture has given way to a more functional and often modernistic architectural style. With the larger buildings made possible by increased wealth went more form and elaborate ritual involving robed choirs, gowned ministers and paid soloists. Worship became more objective and liturgical, and symbolism was revived. The decade of depression after 1929 brought this building boom to an end for a time, but it was renewed again in the fifties to meet the spiritual needs of the middle class, who fled from the cities to the surrounding suburbs.

The Churches and Depression

Although the depression began with the stock market crash in October, 1929, its full impact was not realized until after the election of 1932. Congregations with large building debts faced foreclosure. Church membership declined in the face of religious disillusionment to which churches fell victim with the loss of their gains and often their property. Missionary giving declined also, and missionary effort was curtailed. The churches did what they could to relieve the economic miseries of members.

Although these tendencies seemed to plague the historic denominations, churches with a Pentecostal, premillennial, evangelistic and holiness emphasis seemed to flourish in storefront meeting places. They won and ministered effectively to the needs of those lower in the economic scale. This tendency has continued through the war-induced recovery and postwar prosperity, so that these more conservative churches are gaining membership faster than many of the larger old-line denominations. In general it may be observed, however, that economic depression and war are not conducive to the development of religious life.

Evangelicals have given more attention lately to economic considerations and especially to the problems of economic justice.

Both the National Council and the National Association of Evangelicals have made pronouncements, although from different premises, on these matters. The former seems to favor more government action and the latter more freedom for the businessman and worker as individuals to apply scriptural principles to economic problems.

The Church Communicates Its Message
in New Ways

Prosperity after two wars has stimulated the tendency to formalism in worship to match the more formal types of church architecture. Divided chancels with a reading lectern and pulpit, services in which more groups use a prayer book, more aesthetic symbolism in worship and a growing literature on worship have been a part of the movement toward dignity in communicating the gospel. The danger of these aids to worship becoming ends in themselves still persists, and the worshiper may confuse the spirit of aesthetic appreciation with vital spiritual worship. Fred Eastman of Chicago Theological Seminary stimulated the increasing use of drama as an aid to worship and to the arousing of religious interest. The use of pageants and dramatizing of Bible stories has increased since the twenties. The Moral Rearmament group has made considerable use of this technique.

G. Stanley Hall at Clark University and John Dewey, with their emphasis upon learning by experience or doing, brought widely accepted changes in both the methods and philosophy of Christian education. Unfortunately, too often the biblical content-centered curriculum gave way to a pupil- and experience-centered curriculum which almost ignored the Bible in favor of ethical and nature-centered studies. Conservatives in recent years have adopted many of the newer methods but have retained the biblical content of graded Sunday school lessons.

Renewed interest in the Bible has been created by such modern speech versions as Goodspeed's Bible (1931), Charles B. Williams' New Testament, J. B. Phillips' New Testament, and the Revised Standard Version, with the New Testament published in 1946 and the Old Testament in 1952. In 1961 English scholars brought out the New Testament section of the New English Bible, and the Lockman Foundation released a revision of the American Standard Version New Testament (the Old Testament to be issued later). Religious literature has also been high on the best seller lists in recent years.

Since the advent of religious broadcasting in 1923, churches have made wide use of the radio to broadcast services as well as special programs, such as the Lutheran Hour, and the Old Fashioned Revival Hour of Charles E. Fuller. National networks have given free time to religious services of inspiration by the National Council and other groups.

The church has also made use of the newer medium of television since 1950. Billy Graham's telecasts of his revival services and Fulton J. Sheen's series are illustrations of effective religious use of this new medium. Christians will have to give greater attention to television as it is now commercially produced and protest individually against its often debasing programming to protect their homes.

The development of moving pictures under religious auspices is closely related. The Lutherans have produced such great films as *Martin Luther*. Billy Graham has made effective use of films as an evangelistic device. Moody Institute of Science has pioneered in films based on scientific principles which are aimed at stimulating life decisions. Numerous other organizations are producing Christian life and missionary films.

Church and State

The proper relationship between the churches and the state is a continuing and vexatious problem which is intensified by the recent demands of the Roman Catholic hierarchy on behalf of their over forty-two million constituents for public aid to education in parochial schools. Many Protestants believe that this demand endangers the historic principle of separation of church and state with a "wall of separation" between the two. In the Everson case, the Supreme Court in 1947 decided in favor of a New Jersey law permitting reimbursement to parents for bus expenses in sending their children to parochial school on the grounds that this was aid to children rather than to a religious organization. Free textbooks and lunches have also been included under this decision, but the proposed grant of federal funds to build parochial schools and to pay teachers seems to threaten gravely the principle of separation of church and state. Protestants and Others United for Separation of Church and State, Paul Blanshard in his writings, and the National Association of Evangelicals have offered bitter opposition to such a move. A related problem has been the teaching by nuns in religious garb in public schools in many states.

The sending of an American ambassador to the Vatican has also been a matter of contention. Informal relations were conducted by a mission to the Vatican between 1848 and 1867, and again in World War II Myron Taylor was sent as Franklin D. Roosevelt's personal representative to the Vatican from 1939 until 1950. A determined Protestant protest prevented the appointment of Mark Clark as United States ambassador to the Vatican when President Truman presented his name to the Senate in 1951.

The legality of released time for religious instruction during the school day in school buildings was challenged by Mrs. Vashti McCollum in 1945 on the grounds of discrimination against her son. The Supreme Court in 1948 ruled against religious instruction in public school buildings. Because it did not ban religious instruction in buildings outside the school, classes in religion have been held in churches in dismissed time granted by the public schools. Further decisions in 1963 have banned the use of the Bible and prayer in the public schools. All these problems demand vigilance on the part of the churches to safeguard the historic principle of separation of church and state.

Other problems call for action by Christians. The family seems to be disintegrating under the effects of modern society as the school is left to take over more responsibility for rearing the child; as economic need or desire for extra luxuries puts both parents to work; and as divorce, alcoholism and delinquency bring problems to many families. The possible role of birth control in the world population explosion calls for consideration. The Roman Catholic church has been adamantly opposed to any artificial devices to control births, but recent discussion points to the possibility of change in this connection.

Science, which has created implements for total destruction—possibly even of civilization—raises the question of how to bring moral values to the same peak of development as scientific knowledge. This involves the problem of spiritual dynamic to make moral values vital.

The Christian can be thankful that the God who has in times past guided the church in the meeting of crises, when it seemed that she was about to be overwhelmed, will provide new life and creative ability to match the crisis. Perennial renewal of spiritual dynamic by revival in past crises provides hope for the future.

BIBLIOGRAPHY

ABRAMS, RAY H. (ed.). "Organized Religion in the United States," *The Annals of the American Academy of Political and Social Science*. Vol. 256 (March, 1948). Survey of American religion.

CAIRNS, EARLE E. *Saints and Society.* Chicago: Moody Press, 1960.

CHERRINGTON, ERNEST H. *America and the World Liquor Problem.* Westerville, Ohio: American Issue Press, 1922. The story of prohibition.

ECKARDT, ARTHUR R. *The Surge of Piety in America.* New York: Association Press, 1958. A critique of the current cult of reassurance.

HENRY, CARL F. H. *The Uneasy Conscience of Modern Fundamentalism.* Grand Rapids: Wm. B. Eerdmans Publishing Co., 1947.

LAMBERT, RICHARD H. (ed.). "Religion in American Society," *Annals of the American Academy of Political and Social Science.* Vol. 332 (November, 1960). Recent survey of religion in the United States.

MARTY, MARTIN E. *The New Shape of American Religion.* New York: Harper & Brothers, 1959. Contends there is a revival of interest in religion rather than a revival of religion.

———. *Second Chance for American Protestants.* New York: Harper & Row, 1963.

OLMSTEAD. *HRUS.* Pp. 541-547, 553, 554, 556-564, 583-593.

PARKER, THOMAS V. *American Protestantism.* New York: Philosophical Library, 1956. Useful survey of problems still facing American Christianity.

PFEFFER, LEO. *Church, State and Freedom.* Boston: Beacon Press, 1953.

STOKES, ANSON P. *Church and State in the United States.* 3 vols. New York: Harper & Brothers, 1950. A comprehensive treatment of relations between church and state in the United States.

SWEET. *SRA.* Pp. 410-415, 421-423, 441-450.

INDEX

CHRISTIANITY IN THE UNITED STATES

By Earle E. Cairns

Written to inform Americans of their great spiritual heritage, this history of Christianity in the United States compares the closely related spheres of religious and political freedom. It discusses national pride in religious pluralism and the problems created by denominationalism in American churches. It contains a comprehensive survey of the whole scope of Christianity in the United States. Excellent for Bible school, college, and seminary use, and for the general public at Bible conferences or in local study groups.

Writes Dr. Cairns: "The aim of the book is to link information and interpretation in an organization that puts the American church in its secular setting so that students may have a brief, accurate account of the origins and development of American Christianity. Useful primary and secondary books are listed so the student can examine any major area in greater detail."

Earle E. Cairns received his high school and Bible school training in Canada, his A.B. degree from the University of Omaha, his Th.B. degree from the Presbyterian Theological Seminary at Omaha, and his M.S. and Ph.D. degrees in history at the University of Nebraska. He also completed a year of graduate work at the University of Wisconsin. He has taught Bible and Church History in various colleges and seminaries, and for the last several years, has been Chairman of the Department of History and Political Science at Wheaton College, Illinois.

The cover design, Old North Church in Boston, Massachusetts, is used by courtesy of Ministers Life and Casualty Union.

 **A MOODY PRESS PUBLICATION**

30-1375
MP175